Now & Then

New & Selected Poems

Now & Then

New & Selected Poems

Robert Phillips

The Ashland Poetry Press
Ashland University
Ashland, Ohio 44805

Books of Poetry by Robert Phillips

Now & Then: New & Selected Poems

Circumstances Beyond Our Control

Spinach Days

Breakdown Lane

The Wounded Angel (limited edition)

Face to Face (limited edition)

Personal Accounts: New & Selected Poems 1966-1986

Running on Empty

The Pregnant Man

Inner Weather

4 More

8 & 8

Copyright © 1960, 1966, 1978, 1981, 1986, 1988, 1993, 1994, 2003, 2006, 2008, 2009 by Robert Phillips (1938–)

Of the new poems, "Skyscrapers," "D.L.S.," "How I Missed Seeing Judy Garland," and "She" appeared in *The Hudson Review*.

Thanks to Farrell Dyde for word processing the entire manuscript.

All rights reserved. Except for brief quotations in critical reviews, this book, or parts thereof, must not be reproduced in any form without permission of the publisher. For further information, contact the Ashland Poetry Press, Ashland University, Ashland, OH 44805.

Printed in the United States of America

First Edition

Hardcover ISBN: 978-0-912592-65-7

Paperback ISBN: 978-0-912592-64-0

Library of Congress Catalog Card Number: 2008937078

Book cover design by Mike Ruhe

Front cover author photo by Nicholas Eyle

Back cover author photo by Gretchen Stolzenberg

Ohio Arts Council
A STATE AGENCY
THAT SUPPORTS PUBLIC
PROGRAMS IN THE ARTS

Author's Note:
The poems presented here are all I wish to preserve from five decades of writing.
—R.P.

For my wife Judith,
and for Graham, Karen and Chase

Contents

I. From *Inner Weather* (1966)

Sunflowers/3
The Weird Sister/4
Viewing/5
Happenings/6
To Aaron Copland/7
Words for Amy Lowell/8
Thirty-Eight Summers/9
Dandelions/11
Writer-in-Residence/12
Magic/13
John Wilde's "Happy, Crazy American Animals
   and a Man and Lady at My Place"/14

II. From *The Pregnant Man* (1978)

The Skin Game/19
Vital Message/20
The Head/22
The Tenant/25
The Pregnant Man/27
The Empty Man/29
The Married Man/31
Artists/33
Decks/37
The Stone Crab: A Love Poem/39
Daffodils/40
Nursery Rhyme/41
Transfer of Title/42
Scissors Grinder/44
The Stigmata of the Unicorn/46
Chimney-Sweeper's Cry/47

III. From *Running on Empty* (1981)

A Letter to Auden/51
Flatworms/52
Vertical & Horizontal/53
The Mole/54
Running on Empty/55
The Death of Janis Joplin/56
The Persistence of Memory, the Failure of Poetry/57
Everyone Recalls the Saints, But What of the Animals?/58
Middle Age: A Nocturne/60

IV. From *Personal Accounts* (1986)

Inside & Out/65
Here & There/67
Coming Attraction/68
In the Dumps/69
The Announcing Man/71
"A Local Artist"/73
Queen Anne's Lace/74
The Well-Tempered Performer/77
Diane Arbus's Collaborations/79
Heavenly Day for a Do: A Pantoum/85
The Wounded Angel/87
Survivor's Song/90

V. From *Breakdown Lane* (1994)

Face to Face/95
Whereabouts/97
Easy Street/98
On a Drawing by Glen Baxter/100

Breakdown Lane/102
Suburban Interior/104
Letter from the Country/105
Wish You Were Here/106
Baltimore & Ohio R.R./107
Piano Lessons/109
No Consolation/110
Five Bucolics/112
Paradise/116
A Little Elegy for Howard Moss/117
Elegy for an Art Critic/118
Flower Fires/121

VI. From *Spinach Days* (2000)

I Remember, I Remember/127
My Valhalla/129
Early Lesson/131
Gingerbread House/132
The Panic Bird/133
In Praise of My Prostate/134
Cherry Suite/136
A Pretty Likeness of the Life/138
Letter to My Mother/139
Hounds/141
Spinach Days/143
603 Cross River Road/147
Oysters/150
Epistles/151
John Dillinger's Dick/153
Sonata/155
Personals/157
Never Date Yourself/158
Sex/160

Late Reading/161
Instrument of Choice/163
Houston Haiku/164
Two for Amy Jones/166
Compartments/169

VII. From *Circumstances Beyond Our Control* (2006)

The Ocean/175
Ghost Story/176
An Empty Suit/177
Expulsion/179
The Snow Queen/180
Homage: Neruda/181
Variation on Vallejo's "Black Stone on a White Stone"/184
Triangle Shirtwaist Factory Fire/185
Two Twentieth-Century American Monologues/187
Headlines/191
Two for Mister Roscoe/192
Two Adaptations from Red Pine/194

VIII. New Poems (2008)

She/199
Skyscrapers/201
Ballad of the Five-And-Dime/202
Four Shorts/203
"Awesome"/204
Pairs/205
The Lonely Man/207
More Headlines/208
Imaginary Friends/209
Amnesty/211

Soliloquy of a Central Park Horse/212
Vacation Bible School/213
Haiku/214
Persephone Speaks/215
Group Portrait with Pulitzer Winner and a Stranger/216
"A Pale and Shapely Leg"/217
D.L.S./218
How I Missed Seeing Judy Garland/219
The Four Seasons/221

I. From *Inner Weather* (1966)

Sunflowers

How bold, how vivid the sunburst of your bloom.
    Yellow rays, you proclaim the summer
with more exuberance and broom stamina
    than all croaking frogs of the season.
You blazon forth your feverish glow,
    brave blond flames meet and match August,
heat for heat. And how brilliantly you defy
    autumn: Blossoms curl like smoke puffs,
kindled bronze, aglow like rust-dapplings,
    molten orange stains. You stand, backbones
stiffening in the breeze, stalking your ground—
    phoenix of flowers, pillars of fire—
then in umber silence, you burn yourselves out.

The Weird Sister

There was a woman with an awful eye
who brandished a witching wand
("To beat the dogs off with!" she cried),
who walked our world even in wildest weather,
nursing within her lank arm's crook
the doll she'd fashioned from rags. Its
bright button eye was affixed
upon the faded blue-denim comforter
which was our sky. The familiar doll,
the daughter, hung limp and loveless within her grasp.
"Fly for us, oh fly!" we jeered,
come to their unpretty pass.

Together they traveled the country's
concourse, past children who shrieked
and grabbed at tattered skirts which dragged like nets
("Fly, oh fly!"), past brindled cows sweetly chewing grass,
centipede clotheslines flapping legs in dervish dance.
They traveled to where our earth ends
and the sky begins, beyond the Dead End sign
over Hasting's Cliff. ("Fly, oh fly!")

Now she has flown.
No cold mud sucks at her freezing toes.
Her high, curlew cries do not thread the winds
shuttling past windows where drowsy students stare.

The doughty daughter, maimed asymmetrical,
cast aside, sees but pities not the spectacle
of that rock pile which rose up rightly
to smash a witch who could not
fly.

Viewing

They come, who have ever loved death better than peace,
better than love or the incantation of laughter;
delighting in the size of the floral display,
remarking how natural the painted, powdered smile.

Happenings

Rounding the blank corner of my block
I stagger under sudden shock—
red lights flash, arched hose streams,
fire-engine throbs, siren screams...
The head knows it is my house
long after eyes espouse
the truth. The neighbors'.
Someone else.

Disaster rarely clangs and wails
before one's door. It comes quietly, in the mail,
in the slight sigh of brakes that fail.
Swimmers disappear silently as the sun,
the ticker's indifferent click-click stuns,
a mote captured in the X-ray beams
malignant. The telegram's bright collage
does not shout, it whispers
you.

To Aaron Copland
on his sixtieth birthday, 1960

Suffused light focused into brilliance of blazing poppies
sprung forth full grown from sparse Appalachian soil:
You have given us adagios and allegros of feeling that soar
over grazed grasses and glazed glasses of a nation
balloon-bursting with joy and hysteria,
      Shaker, Quaker, farmhand, bigcity Jew—
all are here—sprightly, rightly denim dancing to the groan
and thwack of tractors and threshing machines.
Brazen henna-haired Jazz descends upon a New England town,
assaulting the immaculate and austere moods of sunparlors
and hundreds of stingily-lit, yarn-filled sewing rooms.
      Ascend your podium, Maestro-Composer!
Give the tender land more—more ripe rhythms, plump
music to pleasure a tinseled, troubled day.

Words for Amy Lowell

"They laughed who later shouted praise
for my fruit shops, Chinese jewels,
my flower fragments, dragon scales.
Yet look, look what it all has brought:
Reflections upon reflections,
word-nettings of wind, of silver,
can now startle, sashay—then leap
off the page straight to the mind's eye.
Sing my praises now if you will,
you sycophants and fawning fools;
but be brief as a soap bubble,
concise as any grain of sand."

Thirty-Eight Summers

Helen, her sun-dead skin
tanned umber the three months through,
knew desire as she knew
scorched sands of sundry beaches.

Even the coldness of the outdoor shower
pricking her conscience
could do nothing to cool those coals.
Drumming water against the tin
shower stall was sleet against
her heart's barricade.

Helen, when walking the edge of a fretting surf,
would feel the jab of love, sharp, distinct,
the throb of a bare foot that has run
too quickly over rough, nail-studded boards.

To look at the beach was pain enough:
couples everywhere laughing
beneath the saffron-streaked sky.
It made her dizzy, knotted in the throat.

Helen went crabbing one afternoon.
There was no one to help her bait
her safety pin with the dead fish head.
How she hated the dead fish head:
Its insolent eye razored into her body's marrow.

She recalled dry bleached wigs of seaweed
and raw, raw ribs of whale.
She dropped the frail line
into dark water depths below.

For thirty-eight summers she had known
the moist cool smells of wet cement;
nail-gouged sand and grit from her scalp.
Helen knew everything but the feel and smell
of love, and how to bait a safety pin hook.

Dandelions

Tiny heads popping up, yellow as butter,
   they encroach upon the world's front yard
and gather in gregarious lawn parties
   which seem to arrest the season.

Towheads together bobbing gaily,
   frail effulgence of hyacinthine curls,
their life is a summer of festivals.
   They think that they will live forever.

Yet soon enough light heads are gray,
   in the first thin wind they scatter.
Year after year they teach us
   how soon we disappear.

Writer-in-Residence

Schizoid poet, lumber up College Hill
breathing like a dolphin, looking sad—
too many bottles, too many pills,
too little writing, too little, too bad.

The school you teach for, second-rate,
the pupils you preach at, dull.
Genius-in-residence, desolate,
try to hold conference with fools.

Fawning Circes (wanting to be
writers, not wanting to write)
encircle you at smoky teas:
Bitches in heat, about to bite.

Your last book, last testament, ten years ago
cool critics picked and sheared to shreds.
So smile for students, placate ego and Head,
then homeward drag, to bottle, to bed:

In alcohol books get written,
in slumber fey critics swoon.
Bankrupt poet—gray, balding, stricken—
you wake haggard at dawn in some rented room.

Magic

My magic apparatus, my bag of tricks,
rests in the basement now. Cotton-batting rabbit,
mystical linking rings, multiplying billiard balls,
vanishing silk handkerchiefs, feather bouquets—
the preoccupations of a childhood spirited away—
beckon, Svengali-fashion, still.
The lure of chicanery remains.

Stored there, those pretty deceptions,
those fabulous feats of legerdemain,
should seem tawdry to me now.
All lacquer, gilt and glitter cannot conceal
the illusion of illusions. Only children deceive
and are themselves deceived.
The adult mind discovers the trick.

Any day was a good day to practice my magic.
A corner of the attic was reserved
for the black table, its embroidered silver moons
ordered from some Philadelphia prestidigitator.
I was a moon-gazer night and day!
Hours then disappeared for a boy
behind a necromantic table:

It didn't matter if the boy could not hit
a home run, perfect a flying tackle.
Every day had a false bottom.
The mawking outside could not reach
that enchanted tower with its conjurer.
But magician, charmer, pale wizard,
you practiced your tricks too well:

Sleight of hand must be outgrown.
Mere magic cannot stay the mind.
The boy becomes a man of shopworn tricks,
in a world with no trapdoor.

John Wilde's "Happy, Crazy American Animals and a Man and Lady at My Place"

A portly possum dangles by his tail
from my living-room rafter. He adroitly assails
reality from topside, where inquiring crows nest.
The fox in stony stance upon my chest
of drawers looks stuffed, but his bark of love
is such stuff as dreams are made of.

Brilliant-hued birds and somber bats
fly overhead. Underfoot a domiciled wildcat
bats a ball across my planks, beneath my eaves,
but those furry forepaws' claws are sheathed.
The panoplied armadillo has seized
upon shards of a vase which once I prized—

Oh, the vanity of earthly possessions!
The vase was broken in the animals' procession
that toppled my turvy vanity upon its side.
Which is real? The fox and armadillo, or I?
I think there's a leopard behind that door.
The back door is open still. Are there *more?*

A polar bear lurches to embrace me like a brother.
Wild ducks fly in one window and out the other,
following an inner weather I cannot know.
My house is modest. The plaster falls like snow.
It was my sanctuary, legacy for kin.
What kinship with these beasts, clambering in?

Antediluvian arteries pulse in time and quick
with those of a naked lady, prime and pink,
now prancing in step with the great hornéd stag;
the beat of their marching does not lag,
parading princely across cracked linoleum.
Something in her high society succumbs.

All out-of-doors wants in, all in-of-doors, out.
Something wild in the mildest of us shouts.
These creatures, sniffing in strange civility,
would huddle close and comfort us, if they could.

II. From *The Pregnant Man* (1978)

The Skin Game

Oh to be an onion!
Wonderful translucent
integuments, endless layers
of derma and epidermis,
membrane upon membrane
encircling the secret core!
Search for the heart of the onion
and find still another skin.
Search for the heart of the onion
and find yourself, crying.
The onion never cries.

> I am no onion. My skin
> so thin, stenographers
> type memoranda on it.
> Politicians draw treaties
> upon it, barbarians shear it,
> wear it about hairy shanks.
> Enemies use it to make lampshades
> (and call that my shining hour).
> Hunters track me across the ice
> like Little Eva, and flay me,
> still alive. . .

Last week I bought a wet suit.
I wear it all the time.
I clop down the street in it,
flop down into bed in it.
Tough, rubbery, resilient,
it's like zipping myself inside
a deboned black man's hide.
It's being Huckleberry Finn
inside strong Nigger Jim.
It's not as many skins as the onion,
but it is one more.

Vital Message

The last thing I put on
    every morning is my

heart. I strap it to my
    wrist sheepishly, a man

with expensive friends
    exposing his Ingersoll.

But I strap it.
    Outside my sleeve it ticks

away the Mickey Mouse
    of my days. Some people

pretend not to notice. They look
    everywhere else but.

Some people touch it
    to see if it's warm.

It is. Warm as a hamster.
    One open-hearted friend

tried to give me
    a transplant. It wouldn't take.

I was left with my old,
    bleeding. A critic tried

to boil it in acid. It shrunk
    smaller than a chicken's.

One girl broke it. It crunched
    open, a Chinese cookie.

No fortune inside. One girl
    won it. She pats it,

a regular Raggedy Andy. And its
    worst enemy is me. I want

to eat it. Nail chewers know
    how tempting!—a plump purple

plum just above the wrist.
    It bursts with a juicy sigh.

The skin shreds sweet. No seeds.
    So far I only nibble the edges.

There is more than half left.

The Head

Somewhere between your house
     and my house
I lost my head.

Not Walter Raleigh style,
     but gently—a child's
balloon suffused

with helium,
     adrift on the spring air
a surprised afternoon.

It floated over willows
     washing their hair
in silver pools,

sailed above clouds
     pale as cow's milk.
It drifted toward the city

over steeples and aerials
     prickly as a populous
pincushion. It survived,

and came to rest
     outside your fourteenth-
floor window. It hung

around all day,
     a faithful dog
wanting in.

It peered through
     the dusty glass,
a prurient window-washer.

You were there.
	You never looked up
from your writing

desk. It wondered if
	you didn't care,
or if, miraculously,

you never once
	saw beyond the paper
sea to the blue beyond?

A head has no hands
	to knock with. So
it bunted,

a baby socking it
	to you in the womb.
No response.

At dusk it shrugged
	a neckless shrug,
mooned around the sill,

nuzzled the cool pane,
	a fish lipping
an aquarium tank.

Dank with dew,
	it shivered and dozed.
The sun rose, full of itself,

the head began
	to dwindle. Soon it hung
limp as a spent cock,

without the satisfaction.
	A banner in defeat, it sagged,
fell to the sidewalk

with a slight thud.
    No one picked it up.
Wrinkled, shapeless thing!

Unsightly as a bladder,
    unwanted as a used condom,
children kicked it around

like a dead cat. Dogs shat on it.
    Women dug stiletto heels
into it. Fourteen floors

above it all, you
    ran snow-veined hands
through fiery hair,

selected a virgin
    sheaf of paper, dipped pen
in ice, and wrote.

The Tenant

First you carefully slit
my throat from ear to ear
and pulled the flap way back,
an entrance to the wigwam

of my chest, made semi-
circular incisions beneath
my armpits, then carved clean
down each side. Foot braced

against my pelvis, you ripped
the whole flap down, skinning
this cat from chin to belly.
I was open, an unzipped sleeping bag.

You crawled inside, drew the flap.
It sealed tight and final
as Hansel and Gretel's oven.
Now your games begin:

You tap tap tap on my tired brain
with a little lead hammer
like an aspirin commercial,
my bones clang and bang—

ice-cold plumbing attacked
by some irate tenant.
You voodoo hat pins
into my doll-like heart,

kick against my belly: Feel
the world's largest foetus! See
the world's first pregnant man!
Every bit I eat nourishes you,

you funnel off every drink.
When I fast, you suck my blood.
Already I've dropped forty pounds.
When I sleep, you project old horror

movies in the theater of my skull.
When I wake, you make my eyes mist,
spraying Windex on the mirrors
of my soul. I grind, blind Samson,

while you, a sailor, haul anchor,
pull my guts. You've an open-
ended lease, free heat and water,
the garbage is collected regularly—

I'll never get rid of you.

The Pregnant Man

Alone and at three
A.M. felt the first
twinge but thought
it something I ate
(cucumbers especially
big ones do that,
also radishes), but
at four A.M. the waters
broke, ran for a towel
to sponge the sheets
(what would my wife
say?), at five A.M.
the rhythms started
regular as Lawrence Welk,

at six A.M. called
my doctor but he didn't
believe me, called my friends'
answering services, but
they didn't believe. At six thirty
called a taxi but it
didn't, and at eight
on the button, open
as a bellows, clutching
the bedpost, screaming
between gold inlays,
a duck squeezing out
a Macy's Thanksgiving
parade balloon, gave birth
to an eight-pound blue-
eyed bouncing baby
poem. Spanked it to life,
lay back and had a drink.

P.S.
Two hours later
it died. You know
how it is with poems.
(My last one had two
heads and no heart.)

The Empty Man

A cup before coffee, a shell
    after the scrambled egg,
I am a big nothing
    inside. A hole. A hideous
gaping vacuole. X-rayed, I
    reveal a TV set
after the repairman removes the tube.
    Nothing turns me on.

I tried to fill myself
    with hope. It sprang
eternal, for a little while. But
    there is no future in it.
I tried to fill myself
    with history. But the past
is undeveloped, a thin black film.
    Nostalgia is not what it used to be.

I tried to cram myself
    with literature. I became
a stuffed owl: Dickinson and Dickens.
    Diderot and Sappho, Colette
and Kant, Shakespeare and Etcetera.
    In the end,
they proved indigestible.
    In the end, they turned to shit.

I tried to fill myself with you.
    I funneled all your brunette hair,
brown-eyedness, energy, optimism
    and tits. All inside.
I poured you on. But my ass
    had a hole in it. You leaked
away. Your beautiful essence drained
    like dirty bath water.

I tried to siphon off my best friend.
    His liver, his lights,
his action, his camera. I identified.
    I stole his walk, talk, wink,
stink. I sucked him through a straw.
    I, Dracula, succubus, lived
off him for months. The faster I absorbed,
    the slower I spun:

A running-down top,
    a drunken dervish whirl,
going everywhere, getting nowhere,
    my life staggered to a stop.
A decapitated chicken, it fell
    on its side. Help! I'm a key-
hole without a key. Help! I'm an eye
    without a hook. Can *you* satisfy?

The Married Man

I was cut in two.
Two halves separated
cleanly between the eyes.
Half a nose and mouth on one
side, ditto on the other.
The split opened my chest
like a chrysalis, a part
neat in the hair.
Some guillotine slammed
through skull, neck, cage,
spine, pelvis, behind—
like a butcher splits
a chicken breast.

> I never knew which side my heart
> was on. Half of me sat happy
> in a chair, stared at the other
> lying sad on the floor. Half wanted
> to live in clover, half to breathe
> the city air. One longed to live
> Onassis-like, one aspired to poverty.
> The split was red and raw.

I waited for someone to unite me.
My mother couldn't do it. She claimed
the sissy side and dressed it like a doll.
My father couldn't do it. He glared
at both sides and didn't see a one.
My teachers couldn't do it. They stuck
a gold star on one forehead,
dunce-capped the other.

> So the two halves lived in a funny house,
> glared at one another through the seasons;
> one crowed obscenities past midnight,
> the other sat still, empty as a cup.

One's eye road-mapped red from tears,
the other's, clear and water-bright.
Stupid halves of me! They couldn't even
decide between meat and fish on Fridays.
Then one began to die. It turned gray as old veal.

Until you entered the room
of my life. You took the hand of one
and the hand of the other
and clasped them in the hands of you.
The two of me and the one of you
joined hands and danced about the room,
and you said, "You've *got* to pull yourself
together," and I did, and we are two-
stepping our lives together still,

and it is only when I study hard
the looking-glass I see that one
eye is slightly high, one corner
of my mouth twitches—a fish on a hook—
whenever you abandon me.

Artists

I. Picasso's "Boy Leading a Horse"
after the Portuguese of Zila Mamede

It is a naked horse and a naked boy
   who have nothing at all in their nakedness
except loneliness shared, and dim destiny.

No one knows whether the horse mourns the evening,
or if the boy's mourning somehow touches the horse.

When they draw near they are always withdrawn,
   aloof from that evening to which they belong
(in the gray plane that encloses them).

If from one or the other comes suddenly
clarion call or lamentation, we should know

it is because it is evening for both of them—
   The boy's evening comes with the first shining star,
the horse's with the sight of hay.

Just two in time, more lonely with the dusk.

II. Giacometti's Race
for Herbert Lust

Bone-stack
beanstalk
broomstick
clothespole
gangleshanks;
they are
the thin
man inside
every fat one
who clamors
to climb out.
Every jaw
a lantern,
every face
a lean,
hungry look.
Ancient
violence.
Violent
freshness.
Do not
trust them.
Do not
trust them.
But:
the beauty!
Tapers flicker
in vertical
air! Delicacy
of a hair!
Herring-gut
economy.
Studies
of the minimal.
Learn to
love them.

Water,
not milk.
Rail against
fear of paper
shadows. Teach
survival on
slender means.
Live off
the thin
of the land.

III. Charles Burchfield's World
   for John I. H. Baur

In the late great paintings of Burchfield,
    all nature goes round and around!
        Cornstalks jig, crickets genuflect,
           clouds flap like cawing of crows. Those
        wild Burchfieldian nights! The wind
   is a fleet of shrouds. Disaster
explodes from church-bells' claps, tele-

graph wires all shrill. Lie still, lie still
    and think about fear of the dark,
        the mystery that lurks in the hearts
          of trees, in the guts of all stumps
        in still waters. Why is the air
   so heavy with flowers tonight?
Why the cicada's nerve-music?

The night's alive with idiot eyes
    of houses, a thousand wet houses
        that rot. Look: Frequent the alleys
          the same as boulevards. God is
        what you find under a rock, God
   is the face of a hollyhock
in the late great paintings of Burchfield.

Decks

In the fair fields of suburban
counties there are many decks—
        redwood hacked from hearts
        of California giants, cantilevered
        over rolling waves of green
        land, firm decks which do not
        emulate ships which lean and list,
        those wide indentured boards which
        travel far, visit exotic ports of call.
        No. Modern widows' walks,

these stable decks, stacked with fold-up
chairs, charcoal bags, rotogrills,
        are encumbered as the *Titanic's*.
        They echo Ahab pacing the *Pequod*,
        the boy who stood on the burning,
        Crane's jump into the heart of ice,
        Noah craning for a sign, a leaf...
        These decks are anchored to ports
        and sherries which mortgaged house-
        wives sip, scanning horizons,

ears cocked for that thrilling sound,
the big boats roaring home—
        Riviera, Continental, Thunderbird!
        Oh, one day let these sad ladies
        loose moorings, lift anchor, cast
        away from cinderblock foundations.
        Let the houses sail down Saw Mill,
        Merritt, Interstate. You will see
        them by the hundreds, flying flags
        with family crests, boats afloat

only on hope. Wives tilt forward, figureheads.
Children, motley crew, swab the decks.
       Let the fleet pass down Grand Concourse,
       make waves on Bruckner Boulevard.
       Wives acknowledge crowds, lift pets.
       The armada enters Broadway, continues
       down to Wall. Docked, the pilgrims
       search for their captains of industry.
       When they come, receive them. They harbor
       no hostilities. Some have great gifts.

The Stone Crab: A Love Poem
"Joe's serves approximately 1,000 pounds of crab claws each day."
　　　　　　　　　　—Florida Gold Coast Leisure Guide

Delicacy of warm Florida waters,
his body is undesirable. One giant claw
is his claim to fame, and we claim it,

more than once. Meat sweeter than lobster,
less dear than his life, when grown that claw
is lifted, broken off at the joint.

Mutilated, the crustacean is thrown back
into the water, back upon his own resources.
One of nature's rarities, he replaces

an entire appendage as you or I
grow a nail. (No one asks how he survives
that crabby sea with just one claw;

two-fisted menaces real as night-
mares, ten-tentacled nights cold
as fright.) In time he grows another—

large, meaty, magnificent as the first.
And one astonished day, *Snap!* It too
is twigged off, the cripple dropped

back into treachery. Unlike a twig,
it sprouts again. How many losses
can he endure? . . . Well,

his shell is hard, the sea is wide.
Something vital broken off, he doesn't
nurse the wound; develops something new.

Daffodils

After too short
    days in the house
their petals begin

to furl: banners, beached
    starfish inching
their jaunty legs,

ancient suns
    sputtering out,
aborted swastikas,

old billy goats
    wagging gruff
goatees, Chinese gold-

fish trailing trans-
    lucent fins, feeble
butterflies lifting

broken wings, owl-
    brown moths, dead
on the attic floor.

Nursery Rhyme

I rattle the bars
of my old play pen,
poop-poop in my Brooks
Brothers pants again,
puke mulled Pablum
on carpeted floors,
destroy all my toys
and clamor for more;
suckle the tit
when I tipple,
dentures locked
on the purpling nipple,
cry when I'm hungry,
cry when I'm cold,
cry when I'm sleepy—
I'm forty years old
till they visit!

Nana, Mama,
Auntie dear:
They castrate
with pinking shears.

Transfer of Title

It's mine now. I mash
the accelerator and the Buick
monsters up my expensive hill,

its 1959 dorsal fins
thoroughly outrageous now.
It's a fish out of water.

But new, this Buick looked razzy
as some henna-haired hussy, the mistress
you never had. Dirt-farmer,

dirt-poor, you cashed all your insurance
for it. Mother and Father
thought you'd gone mad.

Grandfather, your last fling
transports me through a world
I'm making, a world you never knew:

a neighborhood where color TVs
flicker sickly through every picture-
window, where *Thunderbirds*

come to roost in every drive.
It's quite the oldest thing
in sight, steel and chromium

symbol of my relative
poverty. But I need it.
Its padded dash is a bosom

to comfort me if I fall.
Its directional signals
wink confidence for me.

This Buick's body is heavy as love.
Who would ever have thought
it would outdrag you?

You, who hoed one hundred rows,
then crowbarred the tin roof
off the garage all in one day?

It still burns hardly any oil,
while you lie hospitalized, anesthetized,
your points and plugs shot to hell.

Scissors Grinder

He
set spring
into motion each year
with his
wheel

No
storms came
down or screens went
up before his
fire-

works
Children ran
to see sparks dance (in-
candescent angels
on pins)

For
nickels and dimes
his rotary righted every
hoe axe mower
marriage

Till
stainless
steel made in Japan
orphaned the ancient
cutlery

Then
no scissors etc.
just children come to love
the wheel with empty
hands

He
went. Never
came back this spring or last.
The seasons cleave to one
another,

don't
change, and
all the just-new knives
are dull, they blunt
the days:

Life,
that old
case of knives,
has lost its
edge.

The Stigmata of the Unicorn
Musée de Cluny, 1975, fifteenth-century tapestries

Tapestry I

Two noblemen, two huntsmen,
        a bray of hounds, and a young prince
trouble the bluebells of Flanders.
        They stalk the miraculous. The tracker signals.
Just ahead the virtuous beast
        dips his purled horn into a stream.
The waters instantly purify.

Tapestry II

Goat's head, beard and feet,
        lion's tail and pride, the single
knurled horn—from his eye
        an unnatural blue light.
They ring him with their spears.
        He resists till he sees the decoy
virgin. Into their hands he commits
        his life. He falls upon his knees,
lays down his head upon her lap.
        They close in. They crucify.
Oh, the cry of the wounded unicorn!
        It shatters the bluebells.
It glitters in the air!

Tapestry III

Mortal wounds cannot slay.
        The cock crows, the unicorn rises
again, in glory, in a field fabulous with flowers.
        Stigmata glow on a field of snow.
His face spells forgiveness, hope, immortality.

Chimney-Sweeper's Cry
Düsseldorf, 1972

     Black my suit, black my top hat,
hands, face, black all black.
They stare as I pedal past
in a gang of sticks and brooms.
They tread the common stone.
I climb aloft cheerfully, descend
to sunless Hell: soot, char, old bat dung.

     Ah, only the crookleg stork sings
more sweet than I! I am in
my element. There's a school
book proves man is most carbon.
It's in all that twitches!
Earth Mother's hands are pitch.
Fairer flowers spangle blackest soil.

     'Twas the raven Noah first let go—
the raven, not the dove. Bah,
your white hero astride a white steed;
where are horse and hero now?
Lilies for a dead man's chest.
Black is lively, as here as now;
white? A faceless clock. Listen:

     There is a northerly creature,
I know, the Abominable Snowman,
white raging in a whirl of white,
no blackguard's heart so vile as he.
I choose my broom, I lower myself.
Carbon alone becomes immortal diamond.
Alone through Hell Christ comes to shine.

III. From *Running on Empty* (1981)

A Letter to Auden

About suffering you were wrong, Wystan,
you who understood so much of this world,
went askew on its human position;
how suffering occurs, how people react.
It is true that in Brueghel's "Icarus,"
for instance, everything *does* turn away
quite leisurely from the disaster. But:

Who has not seen countless real instances
where crowds, riveted to an accident,
try to save the bodies from the wreckage;
dive icy green waters for the drowning;
weep genuine tears at a stranger's fire?
All had somewhere to get to, but instead,
knowing that there but for the grace of God. . . ,
tarried to share the human condition.

Flatworms

In biology class we decapitated them,
truncating their bodies, too.
We boys had fun; girls cringed or gagged.

Yet within a week, each half gave rise
to a new half, and head as good as new.
Miracle enough the worms survived.

More miracle, their recapitulation.
I named mine John the Baptist, Anne Boleyn,
Sir Thomas More, and Mary Queen of Scots,

and marveled that such wriggling things
accomplished what queens and martyrs could not.

Vertical & Horizontal

Mother grew up in the Blue Ridge,
thriving on the various landscape,
Southern sounds, the thin air.
He married her, brought her heirlooms,
antiques, pretensions back to Delaware,
back to the only town he ever knew
or felt comfortable in. Mother fell
in love with a uniform, not knowing
how uniform life could be.

Ensconced, immediately she felt oppressed
as teacher's wife, and by the heavy air.
(Could a soufflé ever rise in it?)
"It's not so much the heat," she remarked,
"it's the humility." The landscape?
Unrelentingly flat—not one hill
within ninety miles. The natives'
accent? Flat. The townspeople? Flat-
footed. Even the songbirds songed off-key.

Father never noticed—he,
whose favorite catch was flounder.
Every morning for decades she rose,
deflated, a vertical soul snared
within an horizontal landscape,
knowing a steamroller had run over her life.
And once a year Mother returned
to Virginia, head lifted high, and pretended
she never had come down in this world.

The Mole

"There goes the Mole!" Mother cried.
"You children look quick or you'll miss
him!" It was Father, disappearing down
the cellar stairs. Every day he'd retreat
to his radio shack, stay past midnight.

He'd built a rig others envied, came
from miles around to see. Every day
he'd jam the airwaves, ruin the block's TV.
Every day we'd hear him sit before the mike
calling "CQ, CQ calling CQ" to whoever
listened at the other end. He once
claimed to reach Moscow. "Ralph's the handle,
calling from W2CAT, the Old Cat Station—
W-2-CAT-Alley-Tail." He *was* a handsome cat;
Mother once adored him, I know.

But what I'll never know is, Why he'd talk
to any stranger far away and not once
climb back up the stairs to the five of us
to say, "Hello. . . hello. . . hello. . . hello."

Running on Empty

As a teenager I would drive Father's
Chevrolet cross-county, given me

reluctantly: "Always keep the tank
half full, boy, half full, ya hear?"—

the fuel gauge dipping, dipping
toward Empty, hitting Empty, then

—thrillingly!—way below Empty,
myself driving cross-county

mile after mile, faster and faster,
all night long, this crazy kid driving

the earth's rolling surface
against all laws, defying physics,

rules and time, riding on nothing
but fumes, pushing luck harder

than anyone pushed before, the wind
screaming past like the Furies. . .

I stranded myself only once, a white
night with no gas station open, ninety miles

from nowhere. Panicked for a while,
at standstill, myself stalled.

At dawn the car and I both refilled.
But Father, I am running on Empty still.

The Death of Janis Joplin
"Oh, Lord, won't you buy me a Mercedes-Benz! . . ."
October 4, 1970

Because she was a white girl
      born black-and-blue,
because she was outsized victim
      of her own insides,
because she was voted
      "Ugliest Man on Campus,"
because she looked for something
      and found nothing—
      she became famous.

"Tell me that you love me!"
      she screamed at audiences.
They told. Fat Janis wouldn't
      believe. Twenty-seven,
a star since twenty-four,
      she tried to suck, lick,
smoke, shoot, drip, drop,
      drink the world.
      Nothing worked.

Bought a house, a place
      to go home to.
Bought a dog, something to give
      love to. Nothing worked.
Jimi Hendrix died, Janis cried:
      "Goddamn. He beat me
to it!" Not by much. Three weeks
      later she joined him.
      Part of something at last.

The Persistence of Memory, the Failure of Poetry
In 1979, a New York high school music student, Renée Katz, was pushed in the path of a subway train.

The severed hand flutters
      on the subway track,
like a moth. No—

it is what it is,
      a severed hand.
It knows what it is.

And all the king's doctors
      and all the king's surgeons
put hand and stump together

again. Fingers move,
      somewhat. Blood circulates,
somewhat. "A miracle!" reporters

report. But it will only
      scratch and claw, a mouse
behind the bedroom wall. We forget.

At four A.M. the hand
      remembers: intricate musical
fingerings, the metallic

feel of the silver flute.

Everyone Recalls the Saints, But What of the Animals?
for William Goyen

They were here before we were.
We came on the sixth day.
Their numbers are fabulous.
Their names are forgotten.

>Begin with Noah's animals—a pair
>of every living thing that creeps
>or crawls or runs or flies. Imagine!
>The sky dark with wings flapping,
>wide-winged souls, the ground alive
>with creeping, crawling things!

These are totally anonymous.
Many are not. Consider:

>The dove which brought Noah a leaf, a sign.
>The birds Christ released in the temple.
>The camel which went through the needle's eye.
>The ram in the thicket sacrificed for Isaac.
>The Pascal Lamb sacrificed for all the Jews.
>The lion and the lamb which lay down together.

Then consider:

>The two fishes whose bodies fed the multitude.
>The whale which swallowed then rejected Jonah.
>Jesus' donkey which carried him through Jerusalem.
>The good Samaritan's ass which carried the victim.
>The ox and the ass which worshipped at the manger.
>Balaam's ass beaten for balking at an angel. . .

Who can deny they are much
of the Bible's poetry?
Who can deny they are much
of the saint's magic?
Who can deny every saint
must wrestle with his animal?

    These sweet creatures, who did nothing much
    but give, instruct through the ages
    how man, that latecomer, should live.

Middle Age: A Nocturne

The silver tea service
assembles, stands at attention
when you walk by.
Like some lost regiment,
it wears tarnished coats.

The grand piano bares
yellowed teeth as you
give it the brushoff.
You no longer tickle its fancy.
The feeling is mutual.

The liquor cabinet chokes
on dusty bottles. You're forbidden.
In the wines, sediment
settles like sentiment,
like expectations.

You visit your children's rooms.
In their sleep they breathe
heavily. In their waking
they bear new adulthood
easily. They don't need you.

In her dreams your wife sheds
responsibilities like cellulite,
acquires a new habit.
A gaunt nun of the old order,
she bends to a mystical flame.

All the pictures have been
looked at, all the books read.
Your former black mistress,
the telephone, hangs around;
there's no one you want to call.

But early this morning,
in the upper field—
seven young deer
grazing in the rain!

IV. From *Personal Accounts* (1986)

Inside & Out

Upstairs a young man plays
the stereo. From the ceiling
he watches himself dance like a cock.
No one understands him.

Outside the rain scribbles down
into the suburban garden
once ablaze with poppies,
peonies, salvia, impatiens,

seven varieties of loneliness.
Now the plot thickens
with weeds and poison ivy.
The picket fence wants painting.

The young man wants money,
but will not paint or weed.
Before the empty fireplace
the cat bites off a mouse's head.

In the morning kitchen a lemon
slice of sunlight spills
across a woman kneading dough.
Whole wheat, health food—

there is no health in it
for the young man. The bread
she bakes is bitter to the tongue.
It tastes of acrimony.

Downstairs in the master bath
a man sings a song
from the Fifties: *Where are you,
lucky star? Now and forever!*

He would shake down his life
like a thermometer. He dries
his body, thickened like a pudding.
He leaves the mirror steamed—

he's weary of looking at himself.
The house creaks, an ancient sloop
going nowhere. The basement
carries the cargo of their lives.

Outside in the two-car garage
an aluminum rowboat is suspended
like a rocket ready to blast.
It's hung around for years.

Long ago the boy begged his father
to set the two of them adrift.
But the man fears depths,
and could not save them if they overturned.

Here & There

There was that winter a freezing of fire
and in tumbled nights the enlightening
of a pair, side by side, who were not there.
Though they shared a common bed, one flew out
west to San Diego, the other dreamed
a plaid figure on a New Hampshire mare.
From habit they slept spoon-fashion: Yin, Yang.
A transcontinental cold divided.

Their future seemed all of Manhattan's sky-
line, blacked out. Their match could not brighten that.
When spring came, oozing its thaw and its thud,
together they alone walked flowered fields,
stealing a blossom here, a blossom there,
and seeing nothing living, anywhere.

Coming Attraction

It always appears more appealing
    than the film
you've come to see. Carefully edited

(unlike life), it promises promise,
    glamour, escape—
a new Grace Kelly you've never seen,

cool, unruffled, serene as she hangs
    by her capped teeth
from a helicopter blade. The feature

you paid four-fifty for? All talk,
    talk, talk. You explore
the seat beneath your seat—a wad

of old gum, perhaps something worse,
    stuck like a seal,
hardened, all juices dried (like life).

The popcorn which smelled of childhood
    is stale. This motion
picture you are watching, mere light

play upon a silvered screen. It is not
    going to make a motion
to change your ways, it is not going

to give focus to the brief surprise
    which is your life,
it is not going to slide beneath

cold cotton sheets. No matter how
    often you come back,
you go home more alone than before.

In the Dumps
for Howard Moss

On the back seat, six plastic bags,
securely tied, that stink the morning air:
Driving through the woods to Fireplace Road,
the world is too much with you, as you think.

Such places are a smoking zoo, mostly rats;
this one, East Hampton's dump, is orderly:
fair-copy manuscript of a fugue by Bach,
a Swiss sanitation engineer's ideal.

Ringed by bayberry acres, one rough alp
consists of bottles, another is tin cans;
that flatbed is newspapers fastidiously stacked.
Beyond, the raw ravine engorges all,

an ungrand canyon. There are no outcast
Frigidaires, truck tires, bedsprings—usual
oddments of uselessness. "Take a dump"
no longer means "to void." Waste is compacted,

renamed, recycled, rising to new life—
Lazarus among the rinds and coffee grounds!
You stare into the heap, in love with its ripe
backside. The twenty-first century is here.

Greedy gulls inscribe the salty air,
cruising their next feed. To them this crap
appears a quilt, patchwork-colorful
(if birds see colors, which you rather doubt).

In Bangladesh—this could be Bangladesh!—
such rotten landfill would be a windfall
to those who never even entered the rat race.
Beauty is in the eye of the beholden.

A man with his dog strolls by, they disappear
as you sort, stack, fold, heave: Loneliness
collapses inward like a beer can crushed
in your hand. Night sweats and low finance.

Sort, stack, fold, heave. All flesh is grass,
not plastic which will see this planet out.
Now as your leave you take permanent leave,
consumer consummately consumed at last.

The Announcing Man

Up in the tower of that Bingo stand,
installing amplifier and microphone,
my father wired the carnival for sound.

August sweat rivered his brow.
He crawled the octagonal structure,
screwed a speaker at every other corner.

Hornets, bees and webs plagued his head.
I was there to help—pass up tools,
hold a washer, do what a small boy can.

Equipment in place, he'd mount the stool,
test the mike: "One, two, three, four—
testing. This is a test. One, two, three,

four," then drop a 78 on the turntable,
throw the switch. The brassy blare
of John Philip Sousa skirled the air.

Then all Sharptown knew it was time,
the annual Firemen's Carnival commences!
Strings of colored lights magicked the sky.

At night my father returned, installed
himself in that tower, to call
till midnight countless Bingo games:

"N-29. G-7. B-13. Bingo? Do I hear
Bingo? Don't destroy your cards, folks,
let's check the winning one. That you,

Cooney? Good to see you! Call 'em out,
loud and clear." There was a merry-go-round,
a Ferris wheel, two raffled Chevrolets

and a freaky sideshow. But the center
of it all was Bingo, the center of *that*,
my Dad. For decades he called the game

that sent happy men and ladies home
clutching satin pillows, Navajo blankets,
fringy boudoir lamps, Kewpie dolls.

Every August the men who ran the stand
gave him pick of the litter.
He furnished our home with Bingo prizes.

Envoi

Every August I miss that carnival
and its announcing man. This typewriter
is my microphone. I amplify as I can.

"A Local Artist"
Henry M. Progar, 1927–1982

Ex-flyboy, you came to us from Pennsylvania
hills, Penn's woods, and found beauty
in the flat farms, swamps, ponds, estuaries
of Delaware. While I was trying to get out,
you dug boot heels in. Your paintings revealed
the riches of abandoned barns, listing wharfs,
the wealth of earth tones: browns, grays, tans.

But I had to have the whole rainbow.
I split that flat scene while you painted it.
Today you are dead at fifty-five, too good
to be called "a local artist" whenever reviewed.
What is a local artist but an artist
who happens to live locally? What has art
to do with geography? Yet your oils

have everything to do with geography.
They view newly the local venue. Hank,
your landscapes are your nimbus, they
and your modest self-portrait—a young boxer
with broken nose in a white tee shirt,
contemplating, as deeply as Aristotle
the bust of Homer, a bird posed upon a stick.

Queen Anne's Lace
Isabella Gardner, 1915–1981

I came to the end of Long Island to gather
thoughts and conclude
some piece of writing or other.
Instead I found this mood:

grief over your sudden departure,
debris of our friendship's growth.
Belle, hours before your death
you called and we spoke. Later

I cried. You'd thanked me for what
I'd not remembered doing. Your purpose,
valedictory. You knew. That night
at the hotel, death gave room service.

Once I dedicated a poem to you
(you never saw it) on autumn crocuses.
Something in their rarity, I suppose,
reminded me of you:

After our one real quarrel, I struck
the dedication. It shames me now,
watching the rain, realizing
your gift was to bestow.

When I came to this Spartan place,
I couldn't take the bleakness,
so picked some Queen Anne's Lace
that choked the graveled ways.

Jarred, it stayed rigorously vital,
and for weeks it reminded me of you—
not autumn, but a summer view—
delicate, indestructible.

Before we really met, I thought:
"Our American Edith Sitwell!"—commanding
in your sweeping cape of night,
imperiously tall, spangly earringed.

Like Dame Edith's, yours too was façade:
Inside, sitting dutifully in the music room
of a parents' Boston home, a little redhead
waited for someone to share a game.

A constellation of blossoms, each individually
stemmed, the blooms *are* lace, naturally,
but also fireworks, diamond clusters,
celestial spiders, snowflakes. So much

intricacy and simplicity! Your love
poems, Belle, one feels approach
their art. Inevitable spontaneity.
Just as these appear not merely white,

but an essence of white and green,
absence and presence, dying and living,
nothing in nature is sure. Like life.
Like Piaf, you had no regrets.

Queen Anne's Lace has no scent.
I remember yours—what was the perfume?
Always the same, feminine, eternal.
I'd know it in any room.

Hidden at the heart of the umbel,
one spot of black, like yours
acquaintances steered clear of,
toward the end. Drink uncovered it.

If removed, placed on white paper,
that dot is perceived as purple.
A touch of the royal?
A *trompe l'oeil?*

I remember best our evenings, a spot
called "Simply Good," where the cuisine
matched the name, and the talk—a riot
of anyone we'd ever known.

We brought wine, the owner had
no license. Taking license,
I told "naughty" jokes. You winced,
then laughed fully. Generous as a weed.

You dazzled, and only the odd friend
knew of the son, lost
somewhere in South America; lost,
too, the daughter in Bedlam; the husband

who kicked you out and married
a younger, only to summon you again,
a lifetime later, on his famous deathbed.
How you agonized that decision—

To go or not to go? You left well enough
alone. Belle, my coconspirator,
you survived, bereft,
haunting the Chelsea as before.

The Well-Tempered Performer

The purpose of art is not the release of a momentary ejection of adrenaline but is, rather, the gradual lifelong construction of a state of wonder and serenity.
                      —Glenn Gould (1932–1982)

I. Syracuse: The Early Sixties

When the Byronic wonder slouched onstage
he ignored his audience and worried
the knobs of his traveling piano bench.
Delicately he twisted left and right.
We thought it'd never strike its proper height.
We waited. It was August, the hall hot:
He wore a dark wool coat, sweater and scarf;
on his fingers were dark fingerless gloves.

When finally he began to perform,
his eyes just cleared the keyboard! How bizarre,
like his singing of the melodic strain,
which quite rivaled the piano.
(One critic: "Mr. Gould was in fine voice.")
But it was as if we'd never heard Bach,
the rhythms incisive as icicles,
the thickets of counterpoint clarified.

Afterward, in the moist receiving line,
he refused to shake anybody's hand
until he encountered Louis Krasner,
resigned now to conducting the local
symphony. "An honor," Gould said, offering
his hand as if it were Lalique: "I have
your recording of the Berg." "Ah, the Berg!
I *commissioned* it." The old man became younger.

II. Toronto: The Early Eighties

Past a pricey gift shop and discotheque,
in a shuttered prison-like studio,
Gould holed-up in a touristy hotel.
Unshaven, paunchy, he greeted bellboys
formally when they delivered his tea.
He slept by day, wrote by night, and ordered
one expensive vegetarian meal
each dawn. Then proceeded to make phone calls.

Phone bills mounted monthly to four figures.
"I live on long distance!" he cried, stopping
to pop a Valium. It distanced him.
His concertizing career was annulled.
He conducted instead a long affair
with the tape machine. He'd tape, retape, dub,
redub, until the work was purified.
On occasion he escaped Toronto,

cruising the Carolina coasts sleekly
by dark Lincoln Continental with phone.
Once he sang Mahler to the polar bears
at the Toronto Zoo; they understood.
"These are the happiest days of my life!"
Stickler for structure, he rerecorded
his coup, *The Goldberg*, exactly twenty
years later. Then his demanding life erased.

Diane Arbus's Collaborations

I work from awkwardness. By that I mean I don't like to arrange things.
If I stand in front of something, instead of arranging it, I arrange myself.
—D. A.

I. *Russian Midget Friends in a Living Room on 100th Street, N.Y.C., 1963*

The couple sit close to one another,
their friend apart. She leans toward
them, hand on knee, show of slip below
cotton housedress. Their faces
are compact and wrinkled, overripe
autumn pears, the room dark as the floor's
linoleum. For a living room,
it is furnished oddly: chest of drawers,
dressing table, folding mirror elephantine
behind the Tom Thumb inhabitants.
The diminutive man sits in a Provincial
chair. On the dresser, a lamp shaped
like a bunny rabbit cheerfully stares.

II. *The Junior Interstate Ballroom Dance Champions, Yonkers, N.Y., 1962*

They pose, suspended in perfect form,
she in waltz-length chiffon,
he in shawl-collar white dinner jacket.
They are not a day over fourteen.
Before them on the ballroom floor
rest twin gilt plastic trophies.
The piano is silent, the folding chairs
are empty, the dance floor is empty,
the stage is empty, but still they hold
their pose, their poise,
smiling emptily as the future.

III. Mexican Dwarf in His Hotel Room in N.Y.C., 1970

Propped in his rented bed, he confronts us
directly, mouth turned up
in opposition to his moustache.
His soft torso is naked, hairless
as a chihuahua. The towel which covers
his foreshortened lower half is grimy
—yet on his head perches a shapely hat!
To make him appear taller? A flair
for fashion? His toenails are pared.
His elbow rests upon a deal night stand
which holds his pint-sized whiskey
bottle, his pint-sized world.

IV. A Family on Their Lawn One Sunday in Westchester, N.Y., 1968

Everything has been formalized. The normal couple
repose upon redwood chaise longues which match.
Between them a redwood table holds a drink,
a wallet, an ashtray, cigarettes. Behind them,
between picnic table and the swings,
their son bends over his plastic kiddie pool.
The trees which line their acres are evergreen.
She lies, eyes closed, hair unnaturally blonde,
face a replica of last decade's movie queen.
He lies with hand across his eyes, shielding
them from the sun, or pressed against
an oppressive hangover? What goes through
their minds? The lawn is thin.

V. Retired Man and His Wife at Home in a Nudist Camp One Morning, N.J., 1963

This is what he worked for all his life,
to sit surrounded by the paid-for possessions,

to relax and answer to no one. He regards the camera
unashamedly, wears only bedroom slippers,
his belly an appendage above his small penis.
His wife sits across the room wearing only sandals,
breasts lolling like eggplants, hands folded
between her legs. On the television her photo,
nude, younger, more slender days.
On the wall above his chair, a painting
of some idealized pinup—Marilyn Monroe
breasts, Betty Grable legs. The human body
is not all that it has been cracked up to be.

VI. A Young Brooklyn Family Going for a Sunday Outing, N.Y.C., 1966

The wife is a beauty, eyebrows and hair
deliberately styled like Elizabeth Taylor's.
She holds a camera, a big pocketbook,
an imitation leopardskin coat, and an infant.
But the forlorn expression! Beside her poses
her husband, more casually attired: pullover,
short zip jacket, unbelted trousers.
His face is good-looking but defeated.
His right hand clasps their young son's,
who clasps his little groin and grins, retarded.

VII. Boy with a Straw Hat Waiting to March in a Pro-War Parade, N.Y.C., 1967

The hat is a boater, the tie is a bow,
white shirt, V-neck sweater, dark suit.
He is the boy next door. On his lapel
he wears one pin and two buttons—
an American flag, a "God Bless America
Support Our Boys in Viet Nam,"
and a "Bomb Hanoi." In his right hand
another American flag.

Behind him a stone building looms,
solid as a bank, or an armory.

VIII. Xmas Tree in a Living Room in Levittown, L.I., 1963

The fringed bouclé sofa and polyester
wall-to-wall are immaculate. The lampshade
retains its cellophane. The star-burst
wallclock reads twenty minutes to one.
Early afternoon. This room is underfurnished:
sofa, carpet, blonde television, coffee table,
and one Christmas tree, trimmed with glass
balls, dripping tinsel. It looks like Sophie Tucker.
Beneath it repose a dozen presents,
richly wrapped. Compensation for the year's
deprivations? To stand it in this low room,
the top of the tree is severely lopped.
Never has a room appeared more lonely.

IX. A Jewish Giant at Home with His Parents in the Bronx, N.Y., 1970

They are conversing, but what has he to say
to them, or they to him? He cannot stand
in their house without stooping.
His mother looks up where his head looms
like the giant in Jack and the Beanstalk.
His father stands business-suited, white pocket
handkerchief. How did this proper couple
spawn a giant? He needs special orthopedic
shoes, leans upon a cane. All they ever asked for
was a nice son to take over the family business,
marry a nice Jewish girl. All they ever wanted
was to be proud. He makes them feel small.

X. Two Men Dancing at a Drag Ball, N.Y.C., 1970

The face of the one who leads is turned away.
His shirt, suit and haircut would be at home
on Wall Street or Mad Ave. The face of his
partner is uplifted—defiant? Proud?
Or resigned to a life which has meaning
only after five o'clock when he can leave
the office, go home, don the gay apparel—
blonde wig, high heels, white gloves,
feathered gown downy as a baby egret.
Around the room they whirl, one manly,
one graceful as a little girl.

XI. Transvestite at Her Birthday Party, N.Y.C., 1969

The impossible hotel room on Broadway
and 100th Street has been decorated
with phallic-shaped balloons. A birthday
cake is centered on the bed. With Mona Lisa
hands folded, she reclines, bewigged,
wearing a short lace negligée, Fredericks
of Hollywood. She smiles, teeth reveal a gap
you could drive a truck through. The party
is the cake, one whore friend, her pimp,
and the photographer. The guests are nowhere
to be seen. The presents are nowhere.

XII. Masked Woman in a Wheelchair, Pa., 1970

Before a brick hospital or school
she is a figure reclining in a contraption
placed out-of-doors. Her useless legs
are blanket-wrapped. One hand clutches
a bag—for trick-or-treat goodies?
The other holds before her face a mask,
hideous and warty. She is the witch

on the watch for children, she is the crone
to whom Hansel and Gretel come.
She is the one whose body is all stove in.

XIII. Young Couple on a Bench in Washington Square Park, N.Y.C., 1965

Two figures twine as one: his denimed thigh
swung across hers, her arm wrapped around
his bare back. They are a lyrical bas-relief
in the neoclassical style. Her expression,
dreamy; his, distracted. Tonight she will open
her thighs to him, his nipples will become
attentive eyes. Tonight they will toss
in the back seat of his third-hand Chevrolet.
Her mother worries. Paris takes Helen from Troy.

XIV. Untitled (1), 1970–71

Do they look this way because
they don't know any better,
or because they want to?
Two matrons, arms linked,
grin wide as jack-o'-lanterns,
wear outlandish flowered bonnets
tied with ribbons under the chin,
knee socks, shapeless cardigans.
Is it Hallowe'en, or are they
residents of an America where
every day is Hallowe'en? They face
the camera with uninhibited
delight. In the picture-
taking process, they collaborate.

Heavenly Day for a Do: A Pantoum
The Terrace, American Academy and Institute of Arts and Letters, May

"Heavenly day for a do!"
        "Here comes the Princeton contingent."
"They got Paul here—what a coup."
        "This punch tastes more like astringent."

"Here comes the Princeton contingent."
        "Mike Keeley and Joyce Carol Oates?"
"This punch tastes more like astringent."
        "That reporter's taking *notes*."

"Mike Keeley and Joyce Carol Oates?"
        "The proceedings were much too long."
"That reporter's taking notes."
        "He looks just like Anna May Wong."

"The proceedings were much too long."
        "Look: there's Buckminster Fuller."
"He looks just like Anna May Wong."
        "A shame about Henry Miller."

"Look, there's Buckminster Fuller!"
        "Isn't there anything to eat?"
"A shame about Henry Miller."
        "His acceptance speech was effete."

"Isn't there anything to *eat?*"
        "Helen's wearing a schmata."
"His acceptance speech was effete."
        "Vassar's his alma mater."

"Helen's wearing a schmata."
        "Oh, Norman's dyeing his hair!"
"Vassar's his alma mater."
        "Watch out for that snake Alastair."

"Oh, Norman's dyeing his hair!"
"They got Paul here—what a coup."
"Watch out for that snake Alastair."
"Heavenly day for a do."

The Wounded Angel
for Marlene Ekola Gerberick

It fell like a stone from the sky.
It lay in our potato field,
alien, injured, whimpering.
Kain and I dropped our hoes and ran

to see what it was cast down there.
At first all we could see were wings.
Then it—he!—sat up in a tuck.
One wing, broken, hung like a hinge.

When he saw us he dropped his head.
Downcast, his eyes soft as a hare's,
would not meet ours. We saw the blood
on his wonderful white garment.

What must an angel think, falling
through the dazzling air, stunned, surprised
to leave his brothers and sisters,
to land on this ponderous plot?

We tried to talk with him. Nothing.
Finally we decided to act.
We made a litter from bean poles,
carried him to town. He was light.

Not many saw us walking there,
it was the Sabbath—most slept or
were at church. (We'd broken the Word
to dig potatoes, Sunday morn.)

The few that saw us saw a sight:
two stocky boys in dark work clothes,
bearing an angel through the town!
His wings dripped feathers like white rain.

Where to, church father or doctor?
He seemed to be leaving this world.
We stopped before the doctor's stoop;
he took one look and was amazed.

He set to work on surgery,
stitched that wing with strong cat gut,
bathed and dressed the prodigious wounds,
indicated the need for rest.

We left the angel lying there,
on a cot in a dark back room
in a cottage roofed with green grass
in our tiny fishing village.

We returned to our fields, silent
with prayer that he would recover.
Dusk, we returned to the doctor's.
But the shy angel was not there.

The doctor said he'd locked the door
to make sure the patient was safe
from any who might come to pry.
Later, when he unlocked it—gone,

the cot and room unoccupied,
except for one feather on the floor,
four feet long, angelically white.
There were no blood spots anywhere.

That was long ago. Kain is dead,
the doctor also. I'm infirm.
"It was some great white bird you saw,"
our wives and villagers chided.

Could that be what happened? Often
Kain and I returned to that field,
scanned the starfields above. Some nights
we stood in a snowstorm all white

as a great floating of feathers.
We felt them brush our face, our soul.
Did we see what we thought we saw?
We hoped to God it might be so.

Survivor's Song

All my good friends have gone away.
      The boisterous flight of stairs is bare.
There's nothing more I want to say.

First was Jean—she thought she was gay—
      drunk nightly on *vin ordinaire.*
All my good friends have gone away.

And where is Scotty B. today?
      So Southern, so doomed, so savoir-faire?
(There's nothing more I want to say.)

Sweet Hermione was third to stray.
      How her monologues smoked the air!
All my good friends have gone away.

Daniel, our beer-budget gourmet,
      no longer plays the millionaire.
There's nothing more I want to say

Except: My world's papier-mâché.
      I need them all—weren't they aware?
All my good friends have gone away.
There's nothing more I want to say.

V. From *Breakdown Lane* (1994)

Face to Face

By age forty we all have
the face we deserve,
someone wrote. Do I deserve
mine at fifty-three?
Start with the nose—
bulbous, red as Clarabel's;
doubtless too many Dewar's.
That's no cure for depression.

Regard the broken veins
roadmapping the cheeks.
"Gin blossoms" W.C. Fields
called his. They wended
so floridly across his face,
no amount of pancake makeup
could hide them from
the camera's inquiring eye.

Speaking of eyes, mine are
slits—little red pig eyes.
The scar by the sinister one,
souvenir of a Christmas
when I was young. Up before others,
in the dark I tripped,
bashed my face directly
across the cast-iron platform

of a gift rocking horse.
Blood would not stop until
Doc drove in three clamps.
The other scar, below that?
Reminder of a chance encounter
with a mugger in a men's room.
He beat me, threatened to "snuff"
me if I called out for help.

Some say I am lucky. I say why
do I still perpetuate teenage
acne in middle age? What
should I do not to lose
fistfuls of hair when I shampoo?
How can I stop skin cancer,
burnt and gouged out of my fore-
head regularly as the solstice?

How can I arrest erosion
in my brow, furrows visible
as the canals on Mars?
Auden's description of his face:
"A wedding cake left out in the rain."
My brow competes with Auden's,
worry lines deepening by debts,
non-paying tenants, legal suits.

Why do all three chins sag?
This A.M. I managed a fresh
glance into the looking-glass.
I saw the face buried within
my face. It is my father's,
my grandfather's, bland, plain
as a pudding. Yet some
say they were handsome men.

Whereabouts
for Richard Howard

Isn't it odd how anyone who disappeared
        is said to have been sighted in San Francisco?
What is it about that city with its steep
        streets that so inclines them?

Consider Judge Crater, snapped by Polaroid
        weeding on his knees in his San Mateo garden.
Or the Brach candy heiress after a quake,
        stuffing currency into a sidewalk crevice,

generous to a fault. Ambrose Bierce is seen
        and heard rehearsing his *Devil's Dictionary*
in a Chinese take-out joint on Grant.
        And that boy with bangs pushing crack

and his buns in Haight-Ashbury? Etan Patz,
        no longer young, eyes cunning and feral.
Jimmy Hoffa, set deep in the cement
        of his ways, emerges from the Sheraton-Palace,

a floozie on each arm. He's come a long way
        from Detroit. And wasn't that Amelia Earhart
boarding the Red Eye at International,
        wearing only one size 9 Cat's Paw shoe?

There's Dick Diver strap-hanging on a cable car,
        Michael Rockefeller atop the Transamerica,
Weldon Kees still contemplating San Francisco Bay,
        '52 Ford on the approach ramp. He never left.

Don't they know we need them all to stay away?
        Our mythology's poor enough even without them.
They must remain precisely as last seen,
        just before fadeout, their famous last scene.

Easy Street

It is always several blocks away,
around a corner, a corner
you probably never will turn.

The people who live there seem ordinary
enough, but richer, their houses
and cars bigger, newer, unfinanced.

Every backyard sports a swimming pool.
The people who live there seem
to sleep just like you and me,

but it is a different kind of sleep,
untroubled by dreams of failed exams,
automobiles skidding out of control.

Their children—there are perfect children—
never complain of having to clean
plates of *paté de foie gras* and filet.

Uniformed maids waltz about bearing
feather dusters, but there never is
any dust. Drains do not clog there,

furnaces never fail. Ladies
of the house wear white satin
just like Jean Harlow, spend hours

on white telephones. Their dogs wear
diamond collars, sleep in dog houses
with conditioned air. Lap cats lap

saucers of heavy cream from Limoges.
The men of course never go to work.
They play the links and clip hedges

against inflation. Hulking as elephants,
armored trucks make home deliveries
of more money. If you ever move there,

lock all your windows and doors.
Everyone wants the same address.
Some will simply kill to get it.

On a Drawing by Glen Baxter

For a few years, I managed to eke out
    a meager living as the Human Yo-Yo.
But I tired of the unnatural activity,

arms folded, legs tucked, head bent,
    going toward the sod like a Duncan Imperial
(those expensive blockheads). Once oriented,

you cannot imagine the effort to reverse direction,
    rotating still, sometimes fighting
nausea, straining to rewind, to rewend

my way back. My act was revolutionary,
    but it made my head spin. And he who sent me
reeling took glee in casting me out faster

each time—wham, WHAM, WHAMMO!—until I thought
    my spine would snap. It's hard on the neck,
too. Oh, the tricks he made me do!

Mastering Cat's Cradle was not easy,
    intricate string designs while suspended
in midair. How humiliating to perform

Walk the Dog down on my knees!
    (He even made me wear a spiked collar
and bark ferociously.) But

the last straw, he urged me to perform
    Around the World. I told him to bugger off.
Now I hear he's latched onto a model

who Glows in the Dark. Befitting one
    so unenlightened. As for me, I'm employed
in a bar as a Dwarf Tossee. I'm small enough,

nearly. I wear helmet, knee and elbow pads,
      the wall is Velcro, so is my suit.
If they're not too drunk and toss me right,

I stick, don't feel a thing, hardly.
      What the hell. After the Human Yo-Yo,
it's an act of downright upward mobility.

Breakdown Lane

I thought it was just a right-hand
lane where traffic that has
to drive slow goes,

or a lane where you can halt, curse,
trip on blinker lights,
and wait for a tow.

Yet here I find myself limping along
in the breakdown lane.
No car, no motorcycle,

just me in my sad sneakers, painfully
gaining no more than three
miles an hour,

an out-of-shape marathon man to whom
no spectator passes Gatorade,
wheezing like a Hoover,

taking in landscapes on each side,
the mathematical precision
of August cornrows,

the clean lines of suburban houses
armored in aluminum siding.
Motorists that flow

past on the left are totally in control.
I thought I saw my successful
brother streak by

steering a Lexus. My wife drifted
by on a float. Evening-gowned,
she's Miss Congeniality.

Father drove a steamroller by, flattening
all wildlife that strayed
in his path.

I'm sure my hated office rival gave me
the finger from an open Porsche.
What really hurt

was when my younger self hot-rodded by,
confident, and never acknowledged
me. No one stops,

I don't want them to, it's my breakdown,
I earned it, I'll just stagger
toward the horizon, not

knowing what's ahead, whether there is
a finish line, or why I am crying
on the shoulder.

Suburban Interior

Sun-streamed afternoons
your apartment is flooded

like the Grand Canal,
the room a chiaroscuro.

Vermicular shadows slide
the walls. Like Venice,

we are suspended in time,
the only movement a drift

of motes, we two adrift
within a vermeil glow.

There is no winged lion,
no muscular gondolier,

but a consolation, church
bells in an empty piazza.

You never mind so much sun.
When you draw the Venetian

blinds, I take it as sign
you want to make love. Segue

into dark, the interior
of the Basilica of St. Mark.

The doves outside flutter
into this single mass.

Letter from the Country

There are too many birds here.
Their singing drives me to distraction,
awakens me at uncivilized hours.

At dusk, peepers—do you know what they are?—
do their quaint thing throughout
the cocktail hour. I could go mad.

Too many tall pines surround this cabin.
They drop shabby brown needles everywhere
and keep the sun from ever coming in.

Too many wildflowers litter the fields.
They think being pretty's enough. It's not.
And seeing one deer is one too many

when missing company of another sort.
So how are things in the hot big city?
You could have answered just one of my letters.

Wish You Were Here

As a top slows, teeters, falls on its side,
vacation stalls to a halt. Rain six days
running, newspapers limp, sand underfoot,
kids frantic—too young for Trivial Pursuit.

TV's broken. The multi-movie house
had something new, but rain drew the tourists:
I circled for miles, there was just no way
to park. Back again, she takes up macramé.

I undertake the unnecessary: shave again,
sort hardware I don't even own.
Cocktails at five, too much looked forward to.
Phone-boothed one night, I call my old flame.

The inadequate mattress receives the blame
for dreams I comprehend in the morning:
My bearded boss fires me without warning.
I drop the ball, lose the JV game.

Baltimore & Ohio R.R.

It's dead as a rail spike, they say.
They even pulled up all the ties
from Wilmington to Virginia. Not even a freight
can get from here anymore. Don't listen to such lies.

A certain kind of train still gets through.
The one that took young Tommy Waller
north to summer camp, Silver Lake, organized
sports. That season he grew three inches taller.

Or the train that brings Grand Mary south,
her annual visit—Grand Mary in the latest fashions,
red fox furs, hennaed hair, matching alligator luggage,
in the Parlor Car sipping Manhattans;

her favorite grandchild, I was mesmerized
by her talk of the Stock Market, famous friends,
horse races, the Stork Club, Broadway. . .
I'm as old now as she was then.

But that's the sort of passenger train gets through.
The one bringing Private First-Class Jack Studley home
from Manila, lots of medals and him still in one piece.
He's met by Mom and Dad and Janet Lee Jones,

whom he will marry. You can't stop a train
like that. Or the one bearing LaVern Purdy's
body. She ran off to Hollywood to become a star,
came home in a pine box, not yet thirty.

Then there's the train carrying the President, his wife.
It stopped on a side rail. We were under his spell
while he spoke. Pre-TV, this was our only glimpse.
We liked him. "Give 'em hell, Harry!" we yelled.

That kind still comes through. They're dirty,
brass unpolished, prickly plush seat cushions
explode dust clouds when you sit down. But
the conductor waves at me when the engine rushes

by, and Laddie—my collie then—runs parallel
to the cars till the train is halfway to Hebron.
Some even say old Mister Register, the telegraph operator,
is holed up inside the boarded-up train station.

His ghostly tappa-tappa-tap electrifies windless times,
recreates signals that don't seem to signify anymore.
Listen! I think I hear the eleven-thirty-four!

Piano Lessons
for Lilian Beaulieu Hopkins

The best times came when we exchanged places
      and she sat before the keyboard, hands poised,
then tore into "Soaring," "Carnival," or
      "The Waldstein." Former pupil of Gebhardt,
fellow pupil with Bernstein, she mumbled
      apologies if she fumbled a trill,
an arpeggio. No apologies
      needed—she filled that long rectangular
room with the first live classical music
      I'd heard. Rubenstein could not have thrilled me
more. As her fingers flew across the grand,
      she was transported to Back Bay Boston
of her girlhood, I was transported to
      any place but where I had to grow up.

No Consolation

I'm not the lucky type, I always say,
I never won a thing in my life. But
that's not quite true. Once, young,
I won something at a Saturday matinee
at Schine's Waller Theater in Laurel,
Delaware. Kids packed the theater for
the drawing, popcorn littered the floor.
Noisily we sat through previews
of coming attractions, newsreels, cartoons,
a Hopalong Cassidy, and a Gene Autry.

Finally the house lights came up
and Mr. Kopf, the theater manager,
ambled onstage, blinking like an owl
behind wire-rim spectacles. He wore
white-buck shoes and chewed gum.
Now, he announced, now was the moment
we all had been waiting for. Now
he would produce a slip of paper
from the goldfish bowl and proclaim
the winner of the brand-new Schwinn

bicycle. From the wings he wheeled
it onstage. It stood propped
on its kickstand: shiny, coveted,
and red. I didn't have a bike;
at twelve I was the only kid I knew
who didn't. Was our family too large,
too poor? Hadn't I begged hard enough?
I don't know. But I remember imagining
me Schwinning my way about town,
a red blur, happy as a boy can be.

Mr. Kopf drew the piece of paper.
It had Billy Prettyman's name on it.
(Billy was the town dentist's son.
An only child, he had two bicycles.)
Kids began to hiss and boo. Billy
didn't mind. He ran down the aisle,
up carpeted stairs to claim what he
believed he deserved. (I never knew
what he did with his other two bikes.
Kept them, I assume—a collection.)

Then Mr. Kopf looked mischievous,
announced the drawing wasn't over.
There was to be a Consolation Prize.
From the wings he produced a sack
of potatoes. Everyone laughed, but
not so hard as when my name was called.
I walked down that aisle as if toward
the guillotine. When he handed me
"the prize," laughter began again.
From orchestra to balcony, derision.

Then I carried that hateful sack home.
It grew heavier with every block,
the potatoes reeked of dirt. I thought
of Jesus writhing on the tree
while Barabbas was set free. I considered
throwing the sack away. But my parents
would hear that I had "won," and I knew
that we could use those potatoes. Sunday,
Mother cooked some in an Irish stew.
It stuck to the roof of my mouth like glue.

Five Bucolics

I. Blue and Gold Poem

Feeling like a hospital intern,
    I carry a stainless steel bowl
across the lawn to harvest the sun-
    flower seeds. For months those flowers
stretched, swayed, nodded, slumbered,
    posturing against an Aegean blue
garage. Their yellow and gold
    contrasted with that blue, composing
their own version of Van Gogh.
    Early fall. All the cardinals
cheep-cheep-cheep, making cheap shots,
    groundfeeders in hopes of a handout.
The sky, less blue than the garage,
    is bored with being sky blue so long.
As I begin to scrape sunflower seeds
    with bare fingers, they ping, pang,
and pong into the metal bowl,
    an aria from Puccini—*Turandot.*
The bowl fills, soon the cardinals will,
    and I shall return to the house
to start the season's first fire,
    and dream of sunflowers in October.

II. Bittersweet

All summer long it lightly rained in the leaves,
    gypsy moth caterpillars working
terrible mandibles, stripping all our trees.
    Only the apple stood refulgent, green.
But up close, it was an articulation of bittersweet,
    a tent of woody vines pitched over bare branches,
a nest of serpents struggling toward the light.
    This apple would bear no apples, another fruit—

orange berries, shocking scarlet flesh and root.
      Bittersweet spreads fast as kudzu,
tendrils restless as moths. Stubby plants,
      they exceed themselves by climbing upon
their neighbors' backs. It was some summer
      in our nude yard, but a false face, camouflage.
Like unrequited love, too much hugging smothers.
      With pleasure and pain I ripped the bittersweet down.

III. Rue

You bought that shrub simply out of pity—
its odd and twisted, yellow-fringed flowers
so hideous, whoever else would buy it?

The teardrop blue leaves smell musty and sharp.
You were cautioned you could contract a rash
just by handling or brushing against them.

Could there ever be a plant less charming?
In literature it symbolizes
repentance: "With rue my heart is laden. . ."

In mythology, it's the only thing
on earth the monster Basilisk could not
wither with one long reptilian glance.

Now all winter, in your dead garden, rue
flourishes, vibrant green, through snow, ice:
tough, tenacious, working hard to be loved.

IV. Persimmons

The first fruit tree
to bear on our acre,
the persimmon tempted,
inexorable orange plums.

I was forewarned
at an early age,
wouldn't wait for
first frost to soften,
transform them,
render them edible.
Like Adam, I was
bidden, succumbed.
One taste is all
it took: That tart,
astringent taste
puckered my mouth
like alum—roof afire,
orifice lined with fur.
I spit: threw the hateful
persimmons away.

Yet so it seems to be
with me. Importunate,
impetuous, taking
cherries before girls
were eager, landing
a plum of a job
in the Big Apple
while quite green,
clamoring to be
the Top Banana,
expecting fruits
of my labor before
they'd been earned.
When will I learn
to wait for time
to ripen everything,
as it ripens
the succulence
of persimmons, hanging
in the chill weather?

V. Forsythia

Wordsworth can have his daffodils.
The host of spring I welcome most
is forsythia. No low-to-the-ground
flower bowing and scraping in the wind;
burning bush, bower of blossoming,
shower of gold, fountains of petals
spraying parabolas into innocent air.
Bernini would have approved.

Impatient for their coming,
you can break branches and force
their festivity unnaturally early.
All that they ask is a little tap water,
not even a place in the sun. Twigs
soaked long enough will produce
hairy roots. Plant these sticks,
a bush will bloom. Forsythia spreads.

Yellow blossoms appear along stems
before green leaves—sufficient oddity.
What of forcing? Against nature?
Ritual for an unready virgin?
Marrow sucked from a kitten's bones?
There is a season for all things.
Beauty should be consummate unfurling.
Let altars remain bare in a cold spring.

Paradise
for Gloria and Daniel Stern

    was living in Beverly Hills—
pseudo-Spanish adobe, swimming pool,
Mexican maid, jacuzzi whirl.
They reached out, picked avocados
off their trees. Odor of orange blossom,
flame of bougainvillea, silver Mercedes
and black Porsche ticked in their drive.
Every morning she rose, drew heavy
damask drapes, and cried:
"Another goddamn perfect day!"
Living in the Garden of Eden,
they wanted out.

    Back in Manhattan,
she jokes, "We traded Beverly Hills
for Beverly Sills, and she retired."
But mornings she rises expectantly,
a Christmas child, opens shutters
to sallow skies, smirched snows,
leaden rain which scribbles down,
meager autumn leaves, August indignities.
Once in winter the postman creaks
through drifts to vocalize,
"Ain't this the pits?" "No,"
she sighs, "Paradise."

A Little Elegy for Howard Moss
1922–1987

Howard, you died so many different deaths.
Once an ordinary mosquito bite
became, in your eyes, sign of Lyme Disease.
In the East, it was all the rage that year.
An occasional headache? A tumor
big as an avocado on the brain.
Your prickly heat? The beginning of AIDS.
You name it, you thought you had it in spades.

So when you fled your classes at midterm,
leaving Houston to see your New York internist,
saying, "I feel strange," we said, "That's Howard!"
Except this time symptoms were genuine.
You had real pneumonia, real phlebitis,
a real spot on your lungs and a real heart
attack that turned you to cement late one night.
Even hypochondriacs have real illnesses.

I miss your astringent humor, Old Sport,
your understating every blessed thing
except your health—that topic was sacred.
And how your mind managed to qualify:
"X is quite masterful in what he does;
but what *is* it he does?" It took the breath.
Now your breath's taken, since last fall shut down,
I still resist the urge to telephone.

That's perhaps the biggest vacuum I feel,
knowing I can't pick up the phone to dish
about this one and that—real people
the creations that fascinated you most.
Yet for all your knowledge of character,
you seemed unaware of the role you played—
fawning of would-be poet sycophants,
dislike of thousands of *New Yorker* rejectees, un-
discerned. You died not knowing who you were.

Elegy for an Art Critic
John I. H. Baur, 1909–1987

I.

Years ago you'd seen on the TV
a commercial for inexpensive cremation.
You signed on. After your death,
your family found the run-down place
in White Plains, a factory of sorts.
A rumpled old man ushered them through.
One daughter asked to view the body
alone. She found you on a table
in a box of the flimsiest wood—
not even pine. It buckled and bowed
like an orange crate. Inside,
you looked none the worse for wear.

But that room was bare and shabby,
the only ornament a reproduction
of a ghastly painting—angels dancing
in a grotto—directly over the box.
It's a wonder you didn't roll,
you who helped set standards of an age.
Your daughter rectified. Reaching
into her bag, she took out some Magic
Markers, began to draw: flowers,
butterflies, cats, dogs, clouds,
rainbows appeared on that humbling box.
Done, she summoned the family in.

II.

It was your independence I admired,
that and your absolute honesty.
Like the time I had you to the house
to apprise my latest proud possession—

a painting by an obscure Englishman
whose work I admired, bought sight unseen
through an auctioneer's catalog.
And when I brought that picture out
and held it before your level gaze,
you took one look, nodded, and declared,
"Perfectly dreadful!" Instead of separating,
you cemented our friendship, fast.

III.

Nothing could pin you down.
Not the tractor pushing snow
which tipped with you on it,
trapping you underneath, pelvis
broken, age seventy-three.
When you didn't come in for supper,
your wife investigated.
You could have frozen to death.
Instead, you navigated a walker
in what seemed like weeks.

Not the jam-packed bookcase
in your city pad, which tipped
when you tried to extricate
a Trollope novel tightly wedged
on that topmost shelf.
With quick reflexes you held
the falling case back with one leg
while leaping aside. A bruise
or two is all you got from that,
cheating a literary way to go.

IV.

Nothing could pin you down,
I thought, unaware of the clogged
left ventricle. You popped nitro-
glycerine daily, after climbing
the train platform. No one saw.
Seventy-eight now, you left your coat
on the train, raced back, found it,
carried it through the station,
panting, were struck to the floor.
Strangers got you to Bellevue.

The doctors couldn't pin you down
to agree to a bypass operation:
"I'll *think* about it," you said,
hooked to five individual monitors.
At midnight the medico on duty
observed all five screens black
out simultaneously. Five never go
at once. He reported a power failure.
There was one, inside you. You did it.
Another feat of absolute will:

Nothing was going to pin you down.
Rather than live a diminished life,
I think you took your exit with grace,
opted for minimum loss of face.
If you couldn't cross-country ski,
couldn't jog around the reservoir,
couldn't come and go to the city,
couldn't garden—then to hell with it!
(Your last aesthetic pronouncement.)
Nothing was going to pin you down.

Flower Fires
to the memory of Muriel Rukeyser, 1913–1980

I.

"The flowers are on fire!"
our dinner guest cried.
I leapt to pull the bouquet
away from the candle's dancing
flame. It licked purple,
white, and red anemones as one
cat affectionately licks another.
A song flew out of the flowers
as night flies out of day.
The room filled with the odor.
Scored blossoms, broken promises.

II.

Decades earlier my mother,
a young girl, attended
a Hallowe'en party
costumed as a flower:
blouse and skirt furled
with yellow cheesecloth
petals sewn by Grandmother.
When she paraded past
the open jack-o'-lantern,
Mother's petals trailed
the lit candle, burst
into blossoms of fire.
Frantically she raced
around the attic room,
body half in flame,
until a quick adult
rolled her in a blanket,
drove her home before
refreshments were served.

III.

One noon in April, nineteen fifty-eight,
the Museum of Modern Art in Manhattan,
one of Monet's *Waterlilies* was destroyed.
Flames ate the dry canvas, ate cool pads
and buds, blossoms and stems, roots and mud
and water, all curling into blisters,
a burning pool, cool currents flowing
into hot fire, thirsting, drinking in
creamy dewy flowers, waterlilies drinking
dark instead of day, forced not into bloom
but oblivion, a phoenix bursting out
of the bushes, singing as it soars upward
toward the great domed bell of noon.

IV.

There are many Monet *Waterlilies*.
I have been surrounded by them
in the Musée de l'Orangerie.
But that is the one I miss,
waterlilies in Manhattan
of my young manhood, just as I miss
fiery Muriel, who first wrote
of the phenomenon of waterlily fire.
Before she died her ample body dwindled,
a flame gasping in the crosscurrent,
going, going, gone. Ashes on a hearth,
ashes in an urn. Her poems still burn.

VI. From *Spinach Days* (2000)

I Remember, I Remember
poem beginning with two lines by Yehuda Amichai

The earth drinks people and their loves
like wine, in order to forget.
But I drink wine to remember.

I remember the day at school I thought
I had appendicitis. My father came,
supported me on both sides to the car,

into the doctor's. For that, when Gabriel
blows his horn, may Father be supported
on both sides to Heaven.

I remember the sensation of first love,
like falling down a mine shaft.
But shafts are dark, and all around

me was light, light, light. Her hair
light, and when we locked together
we were a dynamo generating light.

I remember not knowing what I wanted to do
in life. My ambitions scattered like newspapers
on lawns of people out of town,

until I had the right professor for
the right course. Suddenly I was on course
for what I'd do until the day I die.

I remember the day we were wed. In early
morning I walked down Marshall Street,
wanted to proclaim to everyone I met,

"I'm marrying a woman who makes me laugh,
a beautiful woman good as fresh-baked bread,
pure as a beach where no one walks."

I remember the day our son was born,
the longest day and night and day
of my life—imagine how long for her!

When the nurse brought our son to the window,
I was Robinson Crusoe discovering Friday's
footprint: stranger, companion, friend.

I remember, sometimes more than I care to,
the friend I let down unintentionally,
the brothers I hurt through simple silence,

the mother I didn't call often enough when
she was bedridden, weak as water. I even
remember a dog who wanted to play. I didn't.

I remember the day it was confirmed
one of my friends had been telling
lies about me for years—

they cost me friends, a coveted job.
May his tongue be ripped out
and flung to the crows.

I collect memories the way some collect coins.
The memories fade like constellations at dawn.
Until my next glass of wine.

My Valhalla

Forget the Museum of Natural History,
the Metropolitan or the Smithsonian.
The collection I want to wander in
I call the Valhalla of Lost Things.

The Venus de Milo's arms are here,
she's grown quite attached to them.
I circle Leonardo's sixteen-foot-tall
equestrian statue, never cast, browse

all five-hundred-thousand volumes
of the Alexandrian Library, handle
artifacts of Atlantis. Here are all
the ballads and rondeaux of Villon,

the finished score of the *Unfinished Symphony*.
I read Aristotle's missing chapters
of the *Poetics*, last plays of Euripides,
screen missing reels of Von Stroheims's *Greed*,

hear the famous gap in Nixon's tapes.
There are lost things here so lost,
no one knows they were lost—manuscripts
by the unknown Kafka, far greater

than Kafka's; his best friend obeyed,
shredded every sheet. The cure for cancer
is here: the inventor didn't recognize,
the potion went unpatented...

In my museum no guard watches me.
There are no closing times,
it's always free. Here I can see
what no one living has seen, I satisfy

that within me which is not whole.
Here I am curator not of what is,
but of what should have been,
and what should be.

Early Lesson

Her mother brought her down
to the laundry room. Picking
through the wicker clothes basket
she explained, "You must separate
the colored from the white."
And they did. Their black maid,
ironing in the corner, nodded.

Gingerbread House

"A gingerbread house like the one on the cover is as much fun to make as to look at, and you may be as whimsical as you like with its decoration."
—The Cooking of Germany *(Time-Life Books, 1969)*

The parents assist the children
in assembling the gingerbread house.
Stiff cardboard patterns, spicy cakes
fragrantly baking, fixed young faces.

Windows are cut out with a sharp knife,
shutters and trim outlined with jellybeans.
Parents make sure children don't forget
to make a chimney. A chimney is essential.

How much fun it is! Marshmallow snow,
half-timbering of cinnamon sticks,
shingles of overlapping gingersnaps.
And the final touch—a marzipan Star

of David stuck over the chocolate bar
front door. Its six points will alert
everyone that inside is a wicked witch
who must burn to death in an oven.

Some parents deny the witch, the fire,
the blond, blue-eyed darlings who shoved
the body in, skipped home. No once upon
a time. Everyone lives happily ever after.

The Panic Bird

just flew inside my chest. Some
days it lights inside my brain,
but today it's in my bonehouse,
rattling ribs like a birdcage.

If I saw it coming, I'd fend it
off with a machete or baseball bat.
Or grab its hackled neck,
wring it like a wet dishrag.

But it approaches from behind.
Too late I sense it at my back—
carrion, garbage, excrement.
Once inside me it preens, roosts,

vulture on a public utility pole.
Next it flaps, it cries, it glares,
it rages, it struts, it thrusts
its clacking beak into my liver,

my guts, my heart, rips off strips.
I fill with black blood, bile.
This may last minutes or days.
Then it lifts sickle-shaped wings,

rises, is gone, leaving a residue—
foul breath, droppings, molten midnight
feathers. And life continues.
Then its shadow is overhead again.

In Praise of My Prostate
after St. Anne of Weston, who celebrated her uterus

My internist said you are unnaturally large.
Once chestnut-size, you've expanded, he said,
into a tennis ball. (In my encyclopedia,

you come right between Prosody and Prostitution,
just before Prosthesis—strange bedfellows.)
You are an unruly child, a real pisser.

You are a porn star who climaxes in a golden
shower. Sometimes you just peter out
in dribbles and drabs. You began when I found

blood in my semen, red curled into white,
a viscous Christmas candy cane, whirling
down the drain like blood in Hitchcock's *Psycho*.

I was certain I had the big C. "Does it burn
when you urinate?" "Never." "Do you have
trouble getting it up?" "No, my problem

is getting it down." The doctor lectured:
"Whenever you hear sounds of hooves,
the chances are it's just horses.

But if you're determined to hear a zebra,
or even a unicorn, go ahead. Be my guest."
So I thought just horses. Until I began

to drop buckets of blood, the toilet bowl
cranberry-sauce red. I was scared witless.
I got a second, and a third opinion.

To a man, they all said, "Gastroenteritis."
After weeks of expensive antibiotics,
you became healthy. A healthy horse.

Still enlarged, but no zebra, no unicorn.
I put away mortality, which I'd been lugging
around like a big battered trunk.

Now men everywhere are chanting their escapes,
celebrating their perfect little chestnuts,
perfect pelvic and spinal lymph nodes.

One is driving to Enid, Oklahoma, to get married.
One is shimmying up telephone poles in Germany.
One is a perfumed gigolo in Beverly Hills.

One is a hairy son of a bitch on a cement mixer.
One attempts to teach English to Asians.
One is an Alsatian monk who vowed abstinence.

One throws pizzas over his head on Coney Island.
One implements media-software in Houston.
One is an art student working his way through collage.

And one is me, saying a mantra for you—the Grand Gland.
We drive away the grackle of unhappiness.
We watch football and baseball games,

eclipses, sniff wildflowers, make love, eat
whatever we want, every meal no longer the last
for the (mistakenly) condemned man on Death Row.

No, we'll not pack our bags yet. The hooves
we shivering bastards heard were just horses.
For now, the zebras and the unicorns can wait.

Cherry Suite

She gestured toward the master bedroom suite.
"Solid cherry wood!" Mother said grandly.
Two bureaus, two mirrors, four-poster bed,
night stand, and her personal vanity.

It was the best furniture we owned.
The rest, mere veneer. Weekly she sprayed
that suite with Lemon Pledge, buffed it
till it shone deep and red as Beaujolais.

I was drawn to its many drawers, sliding
as if on casters. Hers contained paste
jewelry, perfumes, prom programs (Jefferson
High 1933, 1934), photos of her smug-faced

aviator brother, a handbag made of beads,
scarves, cosmetics, a desiccated starfish,
my stellar report cards since first grade,
an autographed photo of Miss Lillian Gish.

Besides shirts and suspenders, his held
underwear, PJs, new wallets, socks,
reeking pipes, a porno comic with Dagwood
screwing Blondie, and under his hankies a red

and white box of Trojans: "Young Rubber Co.,
Youngstown, Ohio. Sold for the Prevention
of Disease Only." They smelled like artgum
erasers at my middle school. For comparison

I unrolled one, tried it on, despaired
I would ever fill such a thing. Ten rubbers
in the twelve-pack. The next time I looked,
only seven: Jeez, he's done it to Mother

three times in two weeks! (It never occurred
to me, they've done it three times together.)
He's crucifying her, I thought, on a cherry-
wood cross, just as I had had to bear

his cod-cold indifference. (At school
beer-breathed boys lied about sex.
I knew "nice" ladies didn't do such things.
At church Mother'd deeply genuflect,

afterward have the rector home for tea.)
Yet she seemed none the worse for wear,
warbling, "When its springtime in the Rockies,
and the birds sing all the day," as she'd prepare

pancakes and sausages for her family of six.
Trundled across the globe to make me bourgeois,
the cherry suite's mine today—I'm orphaned.
My performance in bed? At times a faux pas.

But, I never enter that room with its bric-a-brac
without thinking, Mom, Dad, old fuckers, come back.

A Pretty Likeness of the Life

Mother in champagne-colored dress,
        neckline with navy-blue crenelles,
Father in dress-white uniform,
        their heads precisely parallel,

they face the future. "Our wedding
        portrait," Mother proudly averred.
For half a century it dominated the air
        above her cherrywood dresser.

In flattering lighting and pastels,
        they were the picture of connubiality.
Mona Lisa smile and military bearing,
        they could be in *Town and Country*.

Sorting the homeplace after both died,
        I found the individual photographs—
Mother's from a high-school prom,
        Father's a college yearbook—halves

of the composite in their bedroom.
        Friends knew they were wed by a justice
of the peace over Christmas break, but
        only I now knew it was in such a rush,

they didn't pose commemoratively.
        Later mother paid a studio to retouch
what haste and pregnancy disallowed,
        her wedding at last made illustrious.

Letter to My Mother

You helped me pack for that milestone
event, first time away from home alone.
It didn't matter the summer camp was poor—
long on Jesus, short on funds—bordering

a tea-colored lake. No matter we could afford
only two weeks. To help get there I hoarded
months of allowances. I was ten, felt grown,
I finally was going somewhere on my own.

You folded the ironed tee-shirts and skivvies—
you even ironed and creased my dungarees.
In Southern drawl: "And of course you'll dress
for dinner!" you said, packing with the rest

my one blazer, dress shirts, and rep tie.
I didn't protest, I was an innocent stander-by.
(The suitcase was a new brown Samsonite.
Even empty that thing never was light.)

First exhilarating day—after softball, archery,
diving instruction (which I took to swimmingly)—
came rest hour. While others took a shower
or wrote postcards home, I dressed for dinner:

the white shirt, the pre-tied striped tie,
the navy jacket. In process I received a wry
glance from my counselor. The dinner bell tolled,
I felt every bit the gentleman as I strolled

toward the rustic dining room. I entered,
the room exploded with boyish hoots and laughter,
pointing at me, the funniest thing they'd seen.
They still had on their shorts or jeans.

The rest of the two weeks were impossible.
Not chosen for any teams, called a fool,
Mother, I was miserable through and through.
But when I came home I never told you.

Hounds
for Max Eberts

When kennels traveled from all over
for a big dog show at our middle school,
I shyly gravitated toward the boxers—
regal, snaggletoothed, feisty. The *Chronicle*

next day published a picture of me
"demonstrating the breed." (Some owners
kindly allowed us kids to oversee
the competition.) I looked a connoisseur.

At home that week I began my intense campaign.
I wanted a boxer puppy for my birthday.
It was the only thing I wanted, I explained.
I'd take real good care of it, I'd say.

I'd name him Duke if he were a boy,
Duchess if she were a bitch. (A bitch!
I used the word just to annoy
Mother. She grimaced, I was in stitches.)

My birthday finally came, I raced downstairs.
"You're not ready for the responsibility,"
I was told. I fought back the tears,
drowning in injustice, a bad call from the referee.

Years passed. Then one night my beery father
came home with two basset hounds he'd won
in a poker game. I should have liked the pair,
but didn't. Squat hot dogs, hammered-down,

long floppy ears, sad watery eyes,
in no way did they resemble my beloved pet
of fantasies. "Not in my house!" Mother cried.
"They'll ruin the sofas with muddy paws, wet

all over the carpets." Father built dog houses
in the very back of the backyard, a chain-link
fence around them like convicts in a prison house
all year long. My busy father never would think

to exercise them. I totally ignored them.
Mother fed them table scraps and dry kibble.
Perhaps twice in the fall father approached the pen,
opened it and released them. What fribblery!

They howled with joy, ran in circles around the yard.
He snapped leashes on their collars, led the pair
to his car, opened the trunk, pushed them in hard.
Hansel and Gretel in the oven! Was there air?,

I worried. With a wave, off he'd go to hunt.
Dick and Peggy were rabbit dogs, it turned out.
Each time father returned with unfortunate
cottontails, he'd clean them at the kitchen spout,

slitting bellies straight down the middle,
dropping blue guts and bilish black blood
into a galvanized bucket. Mother watched, I bridled.
As he skinned them raw, Father sucked on a Bud.

He forgot about the hounds soon as snow fell,
but I became their personal *chargé d'affaires*—
I let them out, raked their pen, made them squeal
whenever I threw a tennis ball into the air.

The next autumn, body and voice matured,
I surprised myself, accompanied Father and hounds hunting.
I winced when that fired rifle bucked my shoulder—
but shed a skin as easily as rabbits in cleaning.

All winter I hounded Mother to let them inside,
pointing out their neglect was criminal.
No, that was something she couldn't abide.
In the cold, the hounds dreamed of the coming fall.

Spinach Days

The odor of cooking spinach
brings them back: summer
evenings, the world's richest
city, Manhattan before my senior year,

when Cadillacs grew tailfins,
Buddy Holly and the Crickets alarmed
parents, Eisenhower full of wind,
Mamie tippling at the Gettysburg Farm.

A blue-chip ad agency awarded
me an "internship." I was recruited
for a world I could not afford.
In my one wash-and-wear suit,

by day I worked in a skyscraper,
aluminum waterfall a lobby construct,
rooftop restaurant for highsteppers.
I wrote clever copy: HOOVER SUCKS

for a vacuum cleaner client,
PIMPLES CAN MAKE YOU RICH!
to druggists for an astringent.
My boss rebuffed my greatest pitch,

KISS YOUR PAINFUL HEMORRHOIDS GOODBYE,
though called it a good attempt.
By night I sweated in my room at the "Y,"
non-air-conditioned, ten dollars' weekly rent.

The one window overlooked an air shaft,
but not a whisper of air shafted there.
I hung a repro of a Picasso lithograph
to make the cell less austere.

Rickety desk pushed tight against the bed,
but not so tight as my budget—
fifty-two dollars a week divided
between rent, food, books, cigarettes—

not necessarily in that order.
Even then books took precedent:
A secondhand *Sorrows of Young Werther*
at the Strand meant total absence

of lunch. Dinners I was resigned
to the Horn & Hardart Automat.
Cheap entrees revolved behind
glass doors, or the vegetable platter—

any three off the steam table
for a total of forty-five cents.
I thought spinach would enable
me with Popeye's omnipotence.

It was mushy, foul, overcooked,
the water dark as octopus ink.
For the rest, mashed potatoes, crook-
neck squash, or corn. I was delinquent

in the Great Food Chain, but content.
Near payday, no money even for spinach,
I let myself into my aunt's apartment
when she was away, quickly dispatched

whatever was in the Frigidaire,
hoping she wouldn't miss it, or
forgive. Dates were free: Washington Square,
the Cloisters, Natural History dinosaurs,

Lewisohn Stadium concerts where some wag
strung banners, EXIT IN CASE OF BRAHMS.
Summer nights strollers could zigzag
through Central Park without qualm,

or so I thought, amble through Harlem
back to the East Side, my date
swinging her handbag like a pendulum,
past laughing Negroes who'd gravitate

to front stoops. (Not for decades will
we say Blacks, then Afro-Americans,
finally African Americans. Nothing's still,
how many changes in a short life span?)

Spinach brings it back: long showers
at the "Y," simply nothing else to do,
Dark Victory billed with *Now, Voyager*
at the Thalia, monkeys at the Bronx Zoo,

browsing that smorgasbord for bibliophiles,
the Gotham, hoping to catch a rising star.
Never did, only fading James T. Farrell
imbibing at the Biltmore Men's Bar.

(The Biltmore Men's Bar! Even the name
is impossible today. But that was then.
All males, all crème de la crème,
leaned on the mahogany bar like denizens.)

I elevated atop the Empire State,
saw nothing but fog on foggy mist,
like the *White on White* immaculate
canvas at MOMA, postimpressionist;

hung outside gated Patchen Place
waiting for Cummings to cross cobbles,
or Djuna Barnes. Neither showed face.
The White Horse, where Delmore hobnobbed,

I shared a pitcher of martinis (a pitcher!)
with two older, hard-drinking pals
who were paying. I paid—a spectacular
hangover for days left me horizontal.

By August the city was a cement inferno.
My boss promised to get me away
to his family's Nantucket bungalow.
He never asked, not even by Labor Day.

One young man invited me to the Pines,
a place I'd never heard of or been.
Co-workers advised I should decline.
Instead I swam alone at the "Y," chlorine

stinging my eyes. (Stripling-shaped,
one-hundred-fifty pounds dripping wet,
the fat man inside me hadn't yet escaped.
Decades later he scored his upset.)

Hive-like corridors buzzed with queens
(no one knew the word *Gays*) cruising
in BVDs, one café au lait called Josephine
because of his effeminate languishing.

Locked in my oppressive room I wrote
parents dutifully, on sticky sheets
slept intermittently, dreaming anecdotes
of fame. I filled notebooks with meters,

not ads. Lines spilled like cataracts.
On occasion I wonder if I were misled.
But most days I think I would go back.
The spinach. The loneliness. The future ahead.

603 Cross River Road
for Judith

1972: The Land—A Love Letter

This hill and the old house on it
are all we have. Two acres
more or less—half crabby lawn,
half field we mow but twice a year.

Some trees we planted, most gifts
of the land. The pine by the kitchen?
Grown twice as fast as our son. The bald
elm lost the race with my hairline.

The mulberry—so lively with squirrels,
chipmunk chases, and songbirds—
fell like a tower in the hurricane.
My chainsaw ate fruitwood for weeks.

(I stacked the heavy logs by the cellar
door, to be retrieved winter nights
for the fireplace, not knowing it's easier
to burn a cement block than a mulberry.)

The juniper tree, the one that all but
obliterated our view? Men cut it down
to make way for the new well and water
pump. That pump should pump pure gold:

we lay awake engineering ways to get it
paid for. But we'll never leave
this mortgaged hill, we thought.
This land is changing as we change,

its face erodes like ours—weather marks,
stretch marks, traumas of all sorts

and conditions. Last night a limb broke
in the storm. We still see it limn the sky.

Wife, we've become where we have been.
This land is all we have, but this love
letter is no more ours than anyone's
who ever married the land. . .

1982: Autumn Crocuses

Basketing leaves during earth's
annual leavetaking, we've realized
with a start—something's missing.
The autumn crocuses that would spring

each October by these rocks.
No longer here! We never planted them,
but they implanted themselves
on us. Now, for their lack

we are poorer. Purest orchid color,
they astonished amidst the season's
dwindling. Crocus in autumn?
How perverse, to reverse the seasons.

Every year we bore a bouquet
into the house with pride,
surprising guests who'd never seen
their like. They thought them

foreign, remote, inaccessible—
like edelweiss. No vase, glass, or jar
ever contained them. Their soft white
stems always bent, jack-eared blossoms

lolled like heads of old folks
sleeping in rocking chairs.

I read once where their yellow pistils
are a saffron source. For us,

source of satisfaction. Now gone.
A woodchuck? Frost? My failure to care
for bulbs? They were the unaccountable
we thought we could count on.

1992: Farewell to the Blue House

Our favorite time of year was fall.
Autumn crocuses had blazed
in rock gardens like gas flames,
trees painted themselves pumpkin,
apple, fireplace smoke traveled

in the breezes. The fall of leaves
created a cinematic panorama—
the spangled lake blue, bluer
than blue beneath Westchester's
skies. Mornings, Canada geese

vectored down, honking and hunkering
in the lower field. Evenings, deer
leapt stone walls, drank their fill.
In the upper field, wild turkeys
strutted. The peaceable kingdom.

Whenever I tired of the city,
I lost myself in trees.
Whenever I tired of human faces,
I bent down sunflowers,
gazed into friendly countenances.

The sun setting over the reservoir,
orange overcoming bruise-colored clouds—
no one felt luckier to have landed somewhere.
Somedays I felt as if I could walk across that water.

Oysters

One evening we toasted with whiskey sours
below Grand Central, in the Oyster Bar.
We sat at the rail, felt the world was ours.

We ordered some of every kind there are—
the Chincoteague, Box, Cotuit, Wellfleet...
You called their looks slimy, just like catarrh.

I quoted the poet, sounding effete:
"Oh, it was a brave man who first ate one!"
Feeling brave, we proceeded to eat.

We compared sizes, colors, con-
sistencies, all the nuances lovers
can extract from moments of pure fun.

Some we squirted with lime, some we covered
with horseradish or Tabasco. A few,
too salty, we sentenced to be smothered

in chilled cocktail sauce. With great ado
that night I showed you—the novice—the way
to act Mrs. Waters. You took my cue,

raised an oyster high overhead, in play
opened your mouth wide as the gates of hell,
and sucked all the mollusk's juices away.

Darling, you learned that lesson much too well.
You took my copious feast, dumped the shell.

Epistles
Three Somonkas

I.

> *You ask how many*
> *kisses would satisfy me?*
> *Count all the sand grains*
> *on the beach, all the night stars—*
> *their number might satisfy.*

All the grains of sand,
and all the heavenly stars,
would not be enough
to satiate me, my dear.
You must think infinitely.

II.

I cannot tell you
how much last night meant to me.
No one has made love
to me with so much passion,
I count the days till next week.

This is just to say
we won't be meeting again.
You're nothing in bed,
and a man needs his loving.
Please return my ring by mail.

III.

> *I am writing you*
> *from my room in the tower.*
>   *I cannot write poems*
> *anymore, I've said it all.*
> *Why don't you come or write me?*

    Sorry for neglect.
Much too busy writing love
    poems to come visit.
I have a new muse named Bea.
Perhaps you should get a dog?

John Dillinger's Dick

Some say it's pickled
(formaldehyde) in the basement
of a funeral parlor in Indiana.
Some say the mortician
had heard of Dillinger's
legendary endowment—
the gangster's gun molls
and cell mates talked.
When the corpse was delivered
by the F.B.I., the undertaker
couldn't wait for the stiff's
great unveiling. He wasn't
interested in bullet holes
(one in the face was
a matter for makeup).
He undertook to measure
length, circumference:
Even nontumescent
it was monumental.
Why should such a marvel
be buried? The mortician,
with his wife's boning knife,
carved away his fleshly
trophy. No one would know:
When laid out in his coffin
the gangster wore a suit.
Some nights as his wife
slept, the undertaker crept down
to the basement, removed
the red velvet cloth
covering the pickle jar,
switched on the lamp—
the jar brilliantly backlit—
and sat admiring.
A few times he invited
his fellow morticians

to come view his jar.
They joked, speculated
what woman could accommodate
it all. Some days he wished
he'd taken the balls too.
Against all offers,
he wouldn't part
with Dillinger's private part.
Since 1934 it's floated
and danced in its memorial
waters, lifting its great
uncircumcised head, mooning
against the glass. When
will it rise again, source
of so much pleasure
and pain? It was like
Albert Einstein's extracted
brain, said to be dropped
by some doltish technician—
splattered and shattered
on the laboratory floor
before it, too, properly
could be measured. But
no measure in death would do
for such prodigious organs.
Only in life, only in action,
could they reveal all
their awesome capability.

Sonata

I. When You Massage

my back, Love, heaven is in your hands,
healing with your touch.

When you work my back, tightness slackens,
cares dissolve, muscles

unkink. I am one with the sea's cadence,
the earth's revolution,

the heart's engine. You knead me, I need you,
sensual as silk, all flesh

is grass, mine rippling waves of wild grass.
You cure me by caring.

II. "You're Coming Unglued,"

a true friend confided. I replied that,
like a formerly solid antique table,
I was experiencing a certain detachment,

a certain separation, a certain desiccation
at solid joinings that had supported me.
It's not as if I willed it. The climate

in which I find myself was unexpectedly
unfriendly. Given so much heat,
nothing could maintain its integrity.

III. After the Crash

they laid out the wreckage of our disaster,
our love affair, in a cavernous airline hangar.
Experts recovered thousands of discrete pieces,
sonar scans sweeping across the creases
of the ocean bed, hoping to uncover
the source of what went wrong, to discover
a missile, a bomb, mechanical failure, human error.
There were no survivors.

Personals

I'm honest, discreet, and no way a lech.
Staying home with a rented video is just fine.
I'm seeking a friend first, we'll see what happens next.

My definition of fun is not very far-fetched:
Enjoy fishing, four-wheeling, casinos, and wine.
I'm honest, discreet, and no way a lech.

Want face-to-face conversation, no phone sex,
non-smoking, drug-free women—the old-fashioned kind.
I'm seeking a friend first, we'll see what happens next.

I like a lady to let her hair down, get a little wrecked.
I have brown hair, brown eyes, am built along trim lines.
I'm honest, discreet, and no way a lech.

I'm thirty-seven, white, have two teenagers by my ex.
Looking for a lady, any age or race, similarly inclined.
I'm seeking a friend first, we'll see what happens next.

No psychos! (My ex didn't play with a full deck.)
I live on the northwest side, near the refinery.
I'm honest, discreet, and no way a lech.
I'm seeking a friend first. We'll see what happens next.

Never Date Yourself
remark by Rob House

Why not? It increases your chances for a date
on Saturday nights. I'd called every unfortunate

in town, been shot down. So finally I telephoned
myself on my own phone mail, left a high-toned

message: I'd be picking myself up at 8:15.
Took a long shower, struggled into Calvin Klein jeans.

Next Ralph Lauren sport coat, Gucci loafers, no sox.
Reeking Chanel for Men, I felt quite cocksure.

I dropped the Corvette top, drove us to Cinema II.
Ironically, a double feature, both Gerard Depardieu.

Bought us a popcorn dripping with extra butter,
we dived in with both hands, busy as a knitter.

In the dark my left hand held my right,
one thigh touched the other, just slightly.

Between features I had to go to the john.
In the aisle I glanced back, saw me seated alone.

After the show, paused for a smoke in the lot.
Myself lit my cigarette. It was almost erotic.

Then a fern bar filled with Yuppie scum.
We drank double Dewar's, Tweedledee, Tweedledum,

resisted urges to pilot us to the dance
floor. Others doubtless would look askance.

Back home I slowly undressed, just one kiss
on the mouth in the bedroom mirror, dismissed

making love to myself in the looking glass.
(I'm not that kind of guy—I've got more class,

it was only our first date, there's time.)
Next day I leave myself a message: "I'm

glad we went out. I had a ball.
In this postmodern age, everyone dates it all."

Sex

Whenever I have it, I'm never in bed
with just my partner. Parents attend,
tsk-tsking under the sheets. Freud
takes notes at the footboard. Jane Russell,
looking just as she did in *The Outlaw*,
squeezes in, Brobdignagian boobs
for my pillows. Harry Reams sidles up,
crowing about his studlier performances.
Kinsey perches on the headboard, calculator
in hand. The seventh grade teacher
for whom I burned and itched comes,
still patronizing. A junior high cheer-
leader, bouncing on the mattress, sis-boom-
bahs my every position. A neighbor who hangs
black Victoria's Secret undies on the line
is back-to-back. Margaret Mead observes.
Lorena Bobbitt lies spoon-fashion and has
her knife. A high school linebacker
who patted my uniformed butt and barked,
"Nice game, Bobby!" cuddles close, confusing
me. Jerry Springer is videotaping
my grunts and heaves for national TV.
It gets very crowded. It's enough to take
the lead out of a Fort Ticonderoga pencil.

Late Reading
"Omissions are not errors."
               —Marianne Moore, Preface to *Collected Poems*
April 20, 1966

Admiring her work and enjoying
a correspondence (she pronounced
in minuscule of one of my modest
poems, "All lines so veracious!")

we traveled to Washington Square
where she was to read at NYU.
Our expectations were elevated:
She'd be witty, wear her tricorn hat.

It was a frail old woman mounted
the platform slowly, bare of head,
wearing pink and white calico.
Her voice gossamer, she read

terribly, swallowing whole lines,
skipping entire stanzas. These
omissions were errors, the poems
mutilated before a wincing public.

Afterward we queued with students
to shake her hand. When she saw
us with her *Arctic Ox* she chortled,
"My favorite of all!", inscribed it

"For Bob and Judy," but forgot to sign
her name. It was a day of blunders;
a great hitter was striking out.
We left, fans whose home team lost.

It was six more years before she died,
that fabricator of frigate pelicans,

pangolins, sea unicorns, steeple-jacks,
plumet basilisks, paper nautiluses.

But, reader, there is no stumbling
on her pages. On the bookshelf
her poems tick like quartz crystals,
precise as the world's exactest clock.

Instrument of Choice

She was a girl
no one ever chose
for teams or clubs,
dances or dates,

so she chose the instrument
no one else wanted:
the tuba. Big as herself,
heavy as her heart,

its golden tubes
and coils encircled her
like a lover's embrace.
Its body pressed on hers.

Into its mouthpiece she blew
life, its deep-throated
oompahs, oompahs sounding,
almost, like mating cries.

Houston Haiku

I.

Pocked-mocked old pervert,
      the moon, lurks behind hedges
looking for lovers.

II.

The night she first kissed
      his mouth, he was pleased as
a dog with two tails.

III.

Her silicon breasts:
      round, firm, golden, as ersatz
as canned Cling peach halves.

IV.

Trying to love her
      is just like licking honey
from the knife blade's edge.

V.

Talk about the past:
      a cat explaining how to
descend a ladder.

VI.

The frozen rain drop,
      dozing on the death-black twig,
dreams of hurricanes.

Two for Amy Jones

I. A Painting

You placed this bouquet upon the waters.
         Casual flowers meant to cheer. Childhood colors:
pink, yellow, green, blue. Loveable, touching. A starfall.

It is a bridal bouquet tossed away in ecstasy.
         It is a floral tribute never delivered to a talent.
It exists upon a plane beyond ecstasy and talent.

See how it is wrapped in newspaper, floating.
         See how it has nothing to do with news, floating.
See how it is neither above or below, real or unreal.

Surely it is rooted, this bouquet of cut flowers,
         in the feminine soul. But—and don't miss it—
a sailboat. Small, white, it floats just beyond:

the male force billowing and blossoming. Bouquet and boat,
         uniting opposites within the celestial light shining,
within the biggest flower's magical black eye.

Look into the eye of the flower, into the eye
         of God, the I of God. Bouquet and boat, flower and I,
real and unreal, male and female, all have become one.

II. An Eclogue

To reach your peeling, pillared house,
one went down wooded Sorrel Road,
(I'd misheard it as "Sorrow Road." Since then,
I've read, in parts of England, sorrel
is called sorrow). Nothing sorrowful

about you or your home. You hustled about,
begonias and cabbage roses in profusion,
ancestral silver tea service twinkling.
One of your small luxuries, you paid a maid
to keep it shining. Your pink, orange, blue

paintings—Piazza San Marco, Duomo with flags flying,
Venetian cats circling alfresco tables like sharks—
were on every wall, stacked in the hall.
Pictures weren't all you painted. Annually
you'd Jackson Pollock the wooden floors,

vivid dribbles, swirls atop battleship gray.
For a brush you used a chicken feather:
"Nothing but a chicken feather achieves
this delicate effect," you crowed. Your Italianisms
glittered like your service—

risi e bisi, pinot grigio, pensione, bienale...
And how you loved word play! One oil painting
(brassieres flapping on an Italian clothesline)
became titularly, "The Nipples of Naples." You were
a slightly naughty teenager, no octogenarian.

After dark you engaged in drink. "More vino,
Dearie?" you'd ask, helping yourself liberally,
or to a gin martini. Small, you were elfin—
hair dyed chestnut, brocade ballet slippers,
shocking pink or kelly green thrift-shop frocks.

Sympathetic, generous, you surprised me
the way you abused your cat. Thin tabby, female,
loving, you never allowed her into the house,
even in icicle weather. When you went abroad,
no provisions. "She'll catch mice or birds,"

you reassured. You had several husbands, cast out
like cats, and one septuagenarian patrician boy-
friend. Driving you to an event, he argued

over politics, so you popped out of his Mercedes,
trudged home in evening gown in the snow.

Once at a dinner party for eight, you produced
a small chicken, asked me to carve. I quartered it,
sent four plates down the table, asked for the
second chicken. There was none. Retrieving plates,
embarrassedly recarving, I reapportioned.

You painted every day, etched caped Ezra Pound,
cast a bronze bust of Marianne Moore, your idol.
You never abandoned Italian lessons, returned
to Venice whenever a major painting was sold,
refreshing your sense of your special world.

Until you began to fall. First, face down
on Tarrytown Library's stone steps. Next, catching
your heel, a wrought-iron patio chair leg—
breaking your eyeglasses but not your hip.
Your California daughter, concerned, sold your house,

transported you to Escondido, Juniper Street.
I thought Juniper boded well—flourishing
evergreen of your native Northeast, flavoring
in your gin. Your daughter's house
was just across the way. She always looked in.

You set up studio, began to paint an alien
western landscape. Not for long. Your mind drifted,
a bad radio signal—classical shifting to rock.
Books went unread, paintings begun, unfinished.
You entered hospital, never checked out.

Your work not sought now, your New York dealer defunct,
for old time's sake I drive down Sorrel Road.
The rustic road sign should surely be changed.
With you not there, Sorrel transliterates into Sorrow.

Compartments

Which shall be final?
        Pine box in a concrete vault,
urn on a mantel?

Last breath a rattle,
        stuffed in a black body bag,
he's zipped head to toe.

At the nursing home,
        sides drawn to prevent a fall,
in a crib again.

His dead wife's false teeth
        underfoot in their bedroom.
Feel the piercing chill!

Pink flamingo lawn,
        a Florida trailer park:
one space he'll avoid.

The box they gave him
        on retirement held a watch
that measures decades.

The new bifocals
        rest in their satin-lined case,
his body coffined.

Once he was pink-slipped.
        Dad helped out: "A son's a son,
Son, from womb to tomb."

Move to the suburbs.
        Crowded train at 7:02,
empty head at night.

New playpen, new crib,
	can't compete with the newness
of the newborn child.

Oak four-poster bed
	inherited from family—
Jack Frost defrosted.

Fourteen-foot ceilings,
	parquet floors, marble fireplace,
proud first apartment.

The Jack Frost Motel,
	the very name a portent
for their honeymoon.

Backseat of a car,
	cursing the inventor of
nylon pantyhose.

First-job cubicle—
	just how many years before
a window office?

College quad at noon,
	chapel bells, frat men, coeds,
no pocket money.

His grandfather's barn.
	After it burned to the ground,
the moon filled its space.

His favorite tree—
	the leaves return to branches?
No, butterflies light.

Closet where he hid
	to play with himself. None knew?
Mothball orgasms.

Chimney that he scaled
        naked, to sweep for his dad:
Blake's soot-black urchin.

The town swimming pool
        instructor, throwing him in
again and again. . .

Kindergarten play-
        ground: swings, slides, rings, jungle gym.
Scraped knee, molester.

Red, blue, and green birds
        mobilize over his crib,
its sides a tall fence.

Two months' premature,
        he incubates by lightbulbs
like a baby chick.

He is impatient,
        curled in fetal position,
floating in darkness.

VII. From *Circumstances Beyond Our Control* (2006)

The Ocean

I slam earth again and again,
        and again and again. Not as

a pediatrician slaps a newborn
        to generate first breath, but as

a crazed mother slaps and slaps
        to punish a willful child.

I attack with whatever is at my disposal—
        edges of broken shells, sharp glass

shards, whale bones, driftwood planks.
        I join tropical storms, hurricanes,

I erode, surely but slowly, your
        paltry grassy dunes. They will fall.

I send jellyfish to sting, octopi
        to strangle, sharks with awful jaws.

I ingest poor fishermen, handsome sailors,
        I riptide scuba divers, grandchildren.

I erode edifices of affluence
        built—with effrontery—within my gaze.

Remember, I sank fabulous Atlantis!
        Remember, I took the *Titanic* with one thud!

In contempt, I sometimes return
        a single sneaker or a drowned swimmer.

I will win. Already I possess three-quarters
        of your surface. I will not be ignored.

Ghost Story

The one to whom he always felt most close
died, and he could never comprehend why
he felt no loss, no grief, shed not one tear.
He kept her picture close by, a souvenir
of times past, foreign, even a bit quaint.
And years went by and still he felt that way
until one night, a party, she was there
(this was in a dream, but more real than real).
More beautiful than she had been in life,
dressed to the nines, she mingled, made small talk,
and eventually came over to him:
"I've been missing you every single day,"
she said. His tears released, she went away.

An Empty Suit

You can tell he was a big man,
46 Long, sleeves that would hang
below your knuckles, back vent
that would flap below your butt.

You can tell by the fine Italian wool
and cut he was a stylish man.
Not some mail-order or Sears suit,
but a designer label from Neiman's.

You can tell he preferred the subtle:
fabric a minuscule tic-weave,
shaded a smoky dove gray,
any color tie would go with it.

You can tell by the hair-oil stain
inside the back collar he was vain,
or at least well-groomed, a man
for whom appearances mattered.

You can tell he was a smoker,
or socialized with one—two tiny
cigarette burns, one on the right sleeve,
one by the middle button.

You can tell by the small gray stain
to the left of the breast pocket
he hadn't had much time lately
to attend the dry cleaner's.

You can tell by the frayed bottoms
of the trousers he had lost a lot
of weight. They had drooped
till he was walking on his cuffs.

You can tell by the two red pills
in the right-hand jacket pocket—
potent prescription-strength
for pain—he underwent some ordeal.

You hope that's a lipstick smudge
high on the pearl gray silk lining;
maybe he was loved by somebody
who saw him through, you can't tell who.

But you can tell by the fact it hangs
in the thrift shop here, it isn't
the suit he was laid out in,
that once lucky, now unlucky stiff.

Expulsion
Etching, *by Lars Bo, 1962*

for Elinor and Jim Cubbage

Paradise: a Persian word meaning "walled garden."
And the eastward-facing Edenic plot is fenced in
like a rich man's compound. What's the point
of the points on the fence? No one's out there to try
to climb in. Marble lions top posts like bookends.
The garden is circular, overgrown with trees,
including the Tree of Knowledge, lifting limbs
in supplication. Somewhere the subtle serpent lies.

Suddenly the wrought-iron gate swings open
between stone stanchions. From out of the forest
soar myriad fowl, making their own expulsions
in formations like swallows, some large as pelicans,
all ghostly white, as if already grieving their loss.
In the far right-hand corner the beguiled couple
exit. She faces the future, he looks back.
But after this, there is no looking back.

The Snow Queen
for A. S. Byatt

Her bedchamber is white
as a refrigerator, cold
all year as a meat locker.

No meat there. The canopy
over her four-poster bed
is hung with white lace

intricate as snowflakes.
Her windows are frosted,
to keep out the dazzle

of the Northern Lights,
the fun of polar bears
dancing on hind legs.

When she pads barefoot
she never feels the carpet's tickle.
Her nightgown

is white as a winding sheet.
Underneath her pillow
she keeps an icicle,

just in case. Her sheets
are ice floes—white on white—
no cherries in the snow.

She is married to Winter.
It isn't as though she were
locked away by a cold groom.

He'd melt like a snowman
all over that shag carpet,
if she would just let him in.

Homage: Neruda

I. Ode to a Banana
for Jules White

Banana, color of the sun,
happy fruit—curved like a smile—
a sunscape, shape of the hunger-
moon, moon hunger, shape of the boom-
erang, smooth golden scimitar,
your hip is the full curve
of my love's hips, your shape
the shape of my arousal.
Banana, your waxy sheath is
an uncircumcised shegitz,
your hacked-off stump
a Thalidomide baby's arm.

I peel back your skin,
revealing your banananess,
your banana-being. Odoriferous
as honeysuckle, lined with corduroy,
stringy, sliced you become shekels,
coins of the realm. Ripe meat
soft as polenta, sweet as roasted
chestnuts, you are chockablock
with potassium. Cut unripe,
you are green, near-tasteless.
Aging, you develop liver spots,
speckled backs of aging hands.

The Hindus believe you
were the fruit forbidden
to Adam and Eve. Your serrated
leaves covered their abject
nakedness. One bunch of you,
banana, can contain two-hundred
bananas. As Livingston's Stanley

exclaimed, "Long after there is no more
wheat, long after there is
no more barley, long after
there is no more rice,
banana, you will feed us."

II. After Reading *The Book of Questions*

Who tells summer it is time to hang out
its yellowed underwear?

Do you know what the earth
dreams about when it hibernates?

In winter does the robin dream
of returning to your backyard?

Are your dreams digital?
Where do they go when you awaken?

And do the poor keep their dreams
stuffed beneath their mattresses?

What makes the trees so happy,
that their leaves jig in the spring?

How does an orange know it is
an orange, and how to taste like one?

How long have the mumbling waves
been conversing with the seashells?

What do you call a tree that moves
from squirrel to squirrel?

When the cat catches a mouse,
do the surviving mice grieve?

Was that prolonged noise in the night
a party given by the peach pits?

Have you ever heard a giraffe sing,
or seen a hippo dance?

Is quicksand a judgment,
or the earth embracing a lover?

What beverage does Jeffrey Dahmer
drink in hell—boy-blood?

Won't death, in the end, be
an interminable case of insomnia?

Variation on Vallejo's "Black Stone on a White Stone"
— *"Me moriré en Paris con aquacero. . ."*

I will die in Houston in the jungle heat,
in air-conditioned air. I already know the date.
I will die in Houston an amber afternoon,
a Thursday—that nothing day—in August,
that dog-days month, when even the grass is depressed.

I will toy with a poem at my antique desk,
attempting something new, doing it badly,
but at least working, trying to see myself
alone, and I am, except for my Siamese cat
lying supine, soporific in a patch of sunlight.

Robert Phillips is dead. When he assayed
to extricate a book wedged in his overloaded
bookcase, the case fell upon him like a tower,
pinned him underneath in a tomb of hardbacks.
His Siamese stood by the cooling body for hours.

On the Interstate eighteen-wheelers smogged
the urban air. His wife came, said undoubtedly
he died happily, scribbling, then reaching for
a favorite book, getting through August in Houston—
the loneliness, the vaporous heat, the humility.

Triangle Shirtwaist Factory Fire
1911

I, Rose Rosenfeld, am one of the workers
who survived. Before the inferno broke out,
factory doors had been locked by the owners,

> to keep us at our sewing machines,
> to keep us from stealing scraps of cloth.
> I said to myself, What are the bosses doing?
> I knew they would save themselves.

I left my big-button-attacher machine,
climbed the iron stairs to the tenth floor
where their offices were. From the landing window

> I saw girls in shirtwaists flying by,
> Catherine wheels projected like Zeppelins
> out open windows, then plunging downward,
> sighing skirts open parasols on fire.

I found the big shots stuffing themselves
into the freight elevator going to the roof.
I squeezed in. While our girls were falling,

> we ascended like ashes. Firemen
> yanked us onto the next-door roof.
> I sank to the tarpaper, sobbed for
> one-hundred forty-six comrades dying

or dead down below. One was Rebecca,
my only close friend, a forewoman kind to workers.
Like the others, she burned like a prism.

> Relatives of twenty-three victims later brought suits.
> Each family was awarded seventy-five dollars.
> It was like the *Titanic* the very next year—
> No one cared about the souls in steerage.

Those doors were locked, too, a sweatshop at sea.
They died due to ice, not fire. I live in
Southern California now. But I still see

      skirts rippling like parachutes,
      girls hit the cobblestones, smell smoke,
      burnt flesh, girls cracking like cheap buttons,
      disappearing like so many dropped stitches.

Two Twentieth-Century American Monologues

I. Ted Bundy, Stalker Rapist
Gainesville, 1980

The thing of it was,
you looked so handsome
and trustworthy—
such a nice smile.

The thing of it was,
you showed me
a laminated ID card,
said you were Police.

The thing was,
you told me someone
had been arrested
breaking into my car,

did I want to go
down to the station
and press charges?
You'd drive me.

You had a hot car,
smooth, brand new.
Smelled like leather,
a turn-on, like you.

Not far down the road
you pulled over,
quickly handcuffed me,
unzipped yourself,

started waving a pistol,
said you'd blow
my brains all over
the highway if I didn't

do what I was told.
Whatever the reason,
I didn't think you would.
(Your cock was tiny,

soft as a slug.) Somehow
I got the door open,
ran. You didn't fire,
but came after me,

waving a tire jack.
I wore high heels,
couldn't run fast,
thought I was a goner.

Then a VW came along.
I lifted my handcuffed
hands and hollered.
It stopped for me.

I'm one of the lucky ones.
I've seen your picture
in all the newspapers—
No question, it was you.

I've seen your face
most nights in dreams,
big as the harvest moon,
grinning like a goon.

It's the good-looking
ones I distrust most—
the way they try to
sweet-talk their way.

Last week in a bar
a guy walked over,
touched my shoulder.
In the ladies' room

I puked my guts out.
I'll find one so homely
some day, I'll simply
go along with him, okay?

Fifteen years after,
you finally got fried.
Clean-shaven bastard,
inside me you're still alive.

II. Texas Cheerleader Murder Plot
Channelview, 1991

I, Wanda Webb Holloway, haven't asked for much.
I want to live in an all-white neighborhood
in a white house—no peeling paint for me.
I want the grass cut every week, whether it
needs it or not, and I want my house cleaned for me.
I want to be able to afford matching shoes
and handbags from Dillard's and I want the minister
to praise my organ playing on Sunday mornings.

So much for what I want for me. For my daughter,
my thirteen-year-old, I want more. Much more.
I want her to be popular with both girls and boys.
I want her to be the very center of attention.
I want her to be on the Channelview Cheerleading Squad.
I can see her leaping in the air, shaking her blue-
and-white pompoms, shaking her budding bubbies.
I can hear the stadium's roar when she jumps.

Problem is, she isn't blonde. It's as clear as
the nose on your face, they're partial to blondes.
Problem is, she's competing against the daughter
of that bitch who lives in a tract house like this,
hers is no better. My hair's bigger. She thinks
she's better, but she's not. Her bony blonde bitch daughter
doesn't even talk to my daughter at school.

So I have a plan. I don't have much money, but
I have my diamond earrings Buddy Lee gave me.
I'll barter them. I can give up my diamonds
to see that bitch wiped out. Not the daughter,
I mean the mother. If someone snuffs her mother
the night before the big tryouts at school,
that daughter will collapse in a puddle of grief.
I'll take the cheer right out of her leader.

Then my daughter will make the Squad. I have
a list, men willing to do the job. It's only
a matter of who and how. I'd like to snuff both
bitches, but I won't. Wanda Webb Holloway wouldn't
harm a child. I'd like to tell my daughter that
it's me who made her pompoms possible, but
I won't. I'd like to keep my diamonds, but
I won't. There's just no end to a mother.

Headlines

War Dims Hope for Peace.
Plane Too Close to Ground, Crash Probe Told.
Clinton Wins Budget; More Lies Ahead.

Miners Refuse to Work after Death.
Include Your Children When Baking Cookies.
War Dims Hope for Peace.

Something Went Wrong in Jet Crash, Experts Say.
Prostitutes Appeal to Pope.
Clinton Wins Budget; More Lies Ahead.

Local High School Dropouts Cut in Half.
Couple Slain; Police Suspect Homicide.
War Dims Hope for Peace.

Stolen Painting Found by Tree.
Panda Mating Fails; Veterinarian Takes Over.
Clinton Wins Budget; More Lies Ahead.

Iraqi Head Seeks Arms.
Police Campaign to Run Down Jaywalkers.
War Dims Hope for Peace.
Clinton Wins Budget; More Lies Ahead.

Two for Mister Roscoe

I. "Arsh Potatoes"

"Roscoe's strictly a meat-and-potatoes man,"
was how Grandmother described my late grandfather.
There never was a dinner when we went over
without mashed potatoes—a smooth white mountain

heaped in a blue Willowware bowl. He always had thirds,
topped with gravy, which he called "The Essence."
After grace, he'd point: "Bobby, would you commence
to pass the Arsh potatoes?" His very words.

For years that's what I thought they were called—
not Irish potatoes, but Arsh. It was one
of the few things he got wrong. Farmer's son,
he dropped out in seventh grade to work. Prodigious

energies made successes of his tenant farms,
his timber lands, downtown stores, real estate.
Early he amassed a fortune in the aggregate,
was accorded great respect. With his charm

he was reelected Town Council president three
times. He was proud of his resemblance to Harry Truman,
and of his black Buicks, traded in every two
years. Last night we attended a black-tie Country

Club supper. "Country" club? That manicured fairway
in no way resembles the landscape he tamed in his youth.
So I smile, don't worry about being thought uncouth:
"Would you commence to pass the Arsh potatoes?" I say.

II. Grandfather's Cars

Every two years he traded them in ("As soon
as the ash trays get full") he said with good humor,
always a sedate four-door sedan, always a Buick,
always dark as the inside of a tomb.

Then one spring Grandfather took off to trade,
returned, parked proudly in the driveway.
"Shave-and-a-haircut, two bits!" blared the horn.
Grandmother emerged from the kitchen into day-

light, couldn't believe her eyes. Grandfather sat
behind the wheel of a tomato-red Lincoln
convertible, the top down. "Shave-and-a-haircut,
two bits!" "Roscoe, whatever were you thinking?"

she cried. Back into the kitchen she flew.
No matter how many times he leaned on that horn,
she wouldn't return. So he went inside,
found her decapitating strawberries with scorn.

"Katie, what's wrong with that automobile?
All my life I've wanted something sporty."
He stood there wearing his Montgomery Ward
brown suit and saddle shoes. His face was warty.

She wiped her hands along her apron,
said words that cut like a bandsaw:
"What ails you? They'll think you're turned fool!
All our friends are dying like flies—all!

You can't drive that thang in a funeral procession."
He knew she was right. He gave her one baleful
look, left, and returned in possession
of a four-door Dodge, black, practical as nails.

Grandfather hated that car until the day he died.

Two Adaptations from Red Pine

I. Waiting for a Friend
Chao Shih-Haiu, d. 1219

During magnolia season it rains on every vehicle
Mosquitoes swarm around swimming pools and spas
Waiting after midnight for a buddy who won't show
I throw darts with a stranger until closing time

II. Parting from a Friend on a Night in Spring
Ch'en Tzu-Ang, d. 702

While orange smoke insinuates from Pasadena
We raise longnecks in the Ice House
Thoughts like guitars Friday nights
Following an interminable Interstate
The lurid moon goes down on oil derricks
The Big Dipper hangs it up at dawn
The road to Wichita Falls runs so far away
What year will it turn and run back again

Note:
Red Pine is the pen name of writer and scholar Bill Porter, one of the world's most respected translators of Chinese literature.

VIII. New Poems (2008)

She

talked nonstop the moment
you entered her door.
It went on and on
in circles, like someone
peeling an apple,
went on over cocktails,
hors d'oevres, appetizer,
salad, pot roast, coffee, mints;
you put up with it,
she was brilliant, a fine cook,
and lonely; ceaselessly
the monologue was mixed
with vicious nicknames for
her literary contemporaries—
Robert Penn Warren was
Robert Pen Wiper. Babette
Deutsch was Blab-it Deutsch.
Anne Sexton was Anne Sexfiend.
John Updike was John Upchuck.
And so on. The terrible thing,
you'd heard it all before,
the names, bad jokes,
shop-worn gossip,
color of the dress (blue)
she was wearing when they called
to tell she'd won the Pulitzer
forty-some years before.
She was a young woman then,
beautiful; now, she resembles
Benjamin Franklin in drag,
balding, puffing unfiltered Camels.
They've all passed her by,
left her out of textbooks,
anthologies, her collections
out-of-print or remaindered
(BOOKS FOR A BUCK! at The Strand).
She's received no more prizes,

given no more readings,
not elected to the Academy.
She says she doesn't care:
"I'm waiting to hear from
the Nobel Committee. *They'll*
understand." And she waited
until the day she died. When you
read her poems today, she was right.
They're the absolute real thing.

Skyscrapers

The Flatiron Building,
first "scraper," squat,
like a snout.
Today it hardly scrapes the sky.

The Chrysler Building,
still the most beautiful,
most elegant. It points
its tiara toward heaven.

The Empire State Building,
majestic but haughty.
Imperious, indifferent,
scene of the most suicides.

The Twin Towers, doomed,
still speak to one another
but in whispers.
You hear them around nine A.M.

Ballade of the Five-and-Dime

Oh tell me where, in this land of the free,
penny candy in a barrel has strayed?
Where is Angel Hair for the Christmas tree?
Tin wind-up toys that were Japanese-made?
Where's the counter dispenser of Grape-aid?
Turkey lacers, bra extenders, horehound?
Silk ribbons by the yard? Gone, I'm afraid.
Oh, where shall last year's Five-and-Dime be found?

Where are laundry sprinklers, Orange Tangee?
Rubber door knob covers, plastic barrettes?
Potato peelers, Evening in Paris?
Corn Husker's Oil, oilcloth table cloths, say?
Corset laces, Carbona, collar stays?
Try to find a store that keeps them around.
We need all these things—doesn't someone see?
Just where shall last year's Five-and-Dime be found?

And where would a good notions counter be?
Rickrac, needles, thread, buttons in array?
Wooden sock darners, mitten holders, see?
Beaded hair nets, washboards—all betrayed.
Where are the pickup sticks with which boys played?
Denisen Paper in which girls were gowned?
Rubber window wedges—from a lost day!
So where shall last year's Five-and-Dime be found?

Envoi

You won't find one next week or next decade.
No one answers the question I propound,
but I'll ask it again, quite dismayed—
Where, where shall last year's Five-and-Dime be found?

Four Shorts

Cinquain

Here are
three awesome things:
some chiming bells . . . the light
just at sunset . . . the crying of
new babies.

Piñatas

The little angels
look up at the papier-mâché
donkey with expectant
smiles. The little
bastards beat it to death
with wooden bats.

Sequidilla

Our love is like soft mud
    squishing away,
each moist vestige of cud
    left by mismay
    in its array
from choice's dismay
    at wrack of day.

Toyota Tanka

Farewell Toyota,
Faithful vehicle for years.
It came time to trade.
It cuts me to think the thought:
I'm courting a Chevrolet.

"Awesome"

Everything these days is described as
"Awesome." I get a little dent
in the fender of the Honda, the mechanic
says, "Awesome." I get a belly ache,
the doctor says, "Awesome."
The cat has kittens, the boy next door
intones, "Awesome." Is there no other
adjective these days one can use?
It's part of the devaluation of language.

People used to say, "Impressive," "Charming,"
"Exquisite," "Formidable," "Amusing,"
"Eloquent," "Exciting," "Grandiose,"
"Dramatic," "Magnificent," "Superlative,"
"Glorious," "Splendid," "Majestic,"
"Scrumptious." Today everything is "Awesome."

Pairs

Hibiscus and Oleander

Red hibiscus blossom:
An elf's hat.
Gay umbrella.
Inverted lamp shade.
Victrola's trumpet.
Maidenform A cup.
Drunkard's nose.
Testicular cancer.

Like oleander, you are beautiful
but deadly if one consumes you,
blossoms lethal as arsenic.

Yet if one doesn't get involved,
you are miraculous to look at.
One forgets you are coldest winter.

Schwartz and Shapiro

Delmore left everything
in chaos—his life,
his work, his wives.
It was as if he abandoned
an unmade bed.

Karl left everything
very tidy—his estate,
his library, his wives.
It was as if he straightened
a well-made Army bed.

Dusk and Debussy

Dusk. Fireflies are gold
teeth in a gospel singer's
palatial mouth.

So ethereal,
music of Claude Debussy—
perfume for the ear.

The Lonely Man
I don't glow at all.
—Frank O'Connor

I'm lonely for myself.
Not for my high school girl,
or my college buddies,
or my middle-aged lover—
I'm lonely for myself.

I'm lonely for myself
because I miss someone,
someone unknown to me,
someone I may never meet.
I'm losing friends like hair.
I'm lonely for myself.

I'm lonely for myself.
I can't write a poem
and writing is my life,
such as it is, today.
Where is he? Where?
I'm lonely for myself.

More Headlines

Teacher Strikes Idle Kids.
Juvenile Court to Try Shooting Defendant.
Kids Make Nutritious Snacks.

Normal Man Marries Oblong Woman.
Drunks Get Nine Months in Violin Case.
Teacher Strikes Idle Kids.

New Study of Obesity Looks for Larger Test Group.
Two Sisters Reunited After 18 Years in Checkout Line.
Kids Make Nutritious Snacks.

Astronaut Takes Blame for Gas in Space.
Typhoon Rips Through Cemetery—Hundreds Dead.
Teacher Strikes Idle Kids.

British Left Waffles on Falkland Islands.
Man Struck By Lightning Faces Battery Charge.
Kids Make Nutritious Snacks.

Party Celebrates 50 Years of Loveless Marriage.
Audit of V.A. Health Care Finds Millions Get Wasted.
Teacher Strikes Idle Kids.
Kids Make Nutritious Snacks.

Note: "Normal" and "Oblong" are towns in Ohio. "Loveless" is a surname.

Imaginary Friends

In first grade I was positive there were
furry creatures called tisathees.
Every morning we intoned, "My country
tisathee, sweet land of liberty. . ."

In Sunday school we were instructed
an angel told Joseph to take Mary
and the child and flee into Egypt.
I asked, "What happened to the flea?"

I crayoned a picture of haloed Joseph,
Mary and Baby Jesus in back of a plane.
In the cockpit was Pontius the Pilot.
I titled it, "The Flight to Egypt."

For a decade I dreamed of a nubile
farm girl, Wendy Moon. Kate Smith
crooned her abundant charms:
"Wendy Moon comes over the mountain. . ."

At Christmastime when we caroled away
I had a new friend, a portly monk—
Round John Virgin—as in "Round
John Virgin, Mother and Child. . ."

South Pacific I thought a musical
about a genial couple, Sam and Janet.
Didn't Ezio Pinza sing, "Sam and Janet
evening, you will find a stranger. . . ?"

You'd think there were an end to this.
But even in high school I attended
graduation ceremonies convinced I was
the class valid Victorian. (I wasn't.)

Where are they now, my imaginary friends?
I miss good old Sam and Janet, mysterious
tisathees, Victorians, Wendy Moon,
Pontius the Pilot, and of course the flea.

Amnesty

We demand, I repeat, we demand an amnesty.
Free us from cash machines that chew up our plastic.
Free us from plastic that keeps us impoverished.
Free us from phone solicitors who "have a very important message."
Free us from rap music blasted from boom boxes.
Free us from summer films that are all special effects.
Free us from fast food that is making us fat, fast.
Free us from parties where they serve only hummus.
Free us from graffiti on enduring masterpieces.
Free us from smog, acid rain, and global warming.
Free us from cancer and AIDS and Alzheimer's.

Let us walk in the woods again (if we can find a woods).
Let us read a book again (if computers haven't obsolesced books).
Let us feel free as a paper kite in March.
Let us feel free as a manatee in an open channel.

Free us from feeling that Tom has to dress like Dick.
Free us from guilt if Harry wants to dress like Mary.
Free us from identifying with *The Young and the Restless*.
Free us from Martha Stewart's antimacassar lifestyles.
We need to throw open the front and back doors,
let the daisy-breathed breeze blow through our lives.

Give us an amnesty, Lord. Give us a sign.
It'll be the twist in the kaleidoscope that gives us hope.
Forgive our sins of omissions and our sins of commission.
Assure us it is still not too late.

Soliloquy of a Central Park Horse

For decades you saw me clip clop. I was Juliet,
the dappled white with the white tassel. My owner
paid seventeen-hundred dollars for me. I pulled
children and parents for two decades. For a million
tourists, I was what they remembered of Manhattan.
They were not allowed to feed me, though I would have
loved an apple. My owner was kind, but I could have
used more water, hay and salt lick, more rest.
He didn't know any better. He had no horse sense.

One day, old and full of colic, I simply collapsed.
Frantic, he used his cell phone to call the vet.
The vet told him to beat me until I got up.
To get rid of gas and feces. He beat and he beat
with his whip. I could not get up. He beat harder,
children cried, people in the park shouted, "Stop!"
but he would not. Someone called the police.
My owner said he was following doctor's orders.
So the cop said, "Be my guest." I rose, but collapsed.

That's when my owner beat me to death. My last thought
was of my white tassel and pulling laughing children.
What's to become of my owner? He has no money for
another horse. All he can do is drive a horse.

Vacation Bible School

All my friends were at Trap Pond,
swimming. But every summer I had
to go to Vacation Bible School.
When big-eyed Mrs. Abbott had us sing
"We're Back in Vacation Bible School"
while she thumped the black upright,
I rolled my eyes. It was held in
an unair-conditioned Methodist church,
smelled like church and like my grandparents'
house. The chairs were hard as hardballs.
The air was the inside of mother's GE
toaster oven when turned on High.
The teacher was an old man in a black suit
in August. He smelled like Vicks VapoRub
and bad breath, but had a good memory,
especially for my offenses. I couldn't
pronounce Biblical names like Rehoboam
and Shechem. Who cared about Rehoboam
and Shechem? I cared about Babe Ruth
and the breast stroke. He gave me gold stars
for my reports on Solomon, and on the Windows
of Heaven. I wanted to tell him where to
stick his gold stars. The only good thing
was the red bugjuice they served
mid-afternoon. Every afternoon seemed
long as the months before Christmas.
Everyone else was at Trap Pond, swimming.

Haiku

I.

Since my arthritis,
      my back feels exactly like
broken dog biscuits.

II.

Your pledge to me?
      Useless as a prize in
a Cracker Jack box.

III.

Sluggish Land Turtle
      envied flitting Butterfly,
who quickly would die.

Persephone Speaks

If you think you've had it tough, try being the daughter of Zeus and Demeter. Those are hard acts to follow. And if that wasn't bad enough, I married Hades, God of the underworld. Ye gods, that was sheer hell. I boohooed every day.

Of course, I didn't do it willingly. I peacefully was picking petunias one day when Hades seized me and carried me off to his underworld. I couldn't stand the lack of sunlight. I grew pale as a ghost.

My mama was so miserable, she stopped caring about the harvest, and that's why you guys had famines. That was strictly from hunger. I understand this dude named Ivan Mestovic has done a statue called "Supplicant Persephone." Honey, you don't know what *supplicant* means until you've been to hell!

Daddy finally stopped watching TV and got up off his fat ass to come after me. But because that bastard Hades had made me eat a single pomegranate's seed—one tiny little seed!—I couldn't be completely free. I still had to spend three months of the year with that bastard and only nine months with Mama and Daddy. Mama makes a lot of meatloaf and comfort foods, but it doesn't compensate.

And that's why you guys have winter three months every year. Don't blame me.

Group Portrait with Pulitzer Winner and a Stranger

After Albee's reading, caught by vanity,
I took advantage of "a photo opportunity"—
the playwright, some groupie, my student, me,
a conversation piece. At the pharmacy,
prints in hand, I discover their deviltry:

My student, grinning with *jeu d'esprit*,
lifts two V-ed fingers above the honoree,
who raises horns behind his devotee,
who raises horns which cuckold me.
Beware what's behind you that you cannot see,

beware what's before you, surreptitiously.
Doctor Faustus toured in fifteen-ninety-three;
one night actors beheld one devil too many
dervishing in the damnation scene unbiddenly.
Who or what raised hell? Wailing threnodies,

the players fled Exeter. To ensure safety
Edward Alleyn, playing Faust subsequently,
wore a cross. And who *was* that groupie
who horned his way in behind Edward Albee?
(Beelzebub or Old Nick, feigning fraternity?)

"A Pale and Shapely Leg"
after an image by Raymond Carver

He spent days alone or in a bar,
      nights at a nothing job
in a hospital, where he janitored.

One night he entered the autopsy
      room with bucket and wet mop,
discovered a pale and shapely leg

left on the table top. He stared.
      It was the shapeliest leg he'd seen.
She must have been a knock-out

in a miniskirt. After time-clocking out
      he returned, put the pale and shapely
leg in a plastic garbage bag, lay it

across the back seat of his Chevy.
      Once home he arranged it on his bed,
sheet drawn so the leg stuck out,

looking like a beauty luxuriating.
      In the moonlit room it was nacreous,
curved as the tail of a mermaid.

In the moonlit room he thought
      he could hear her sing her song.
She sang it just for him: "I ain't got

nobody. . ." He sat up all night by the bed,
      tossing shots, smoking Lucky Strikes.
The sun came up, as it always does.

He wrapped the disembodied thing,
      chucked it in the Dempster dumpster,
and went on with his life.

D.L.S.

Plucky Donald Lee Smith strutted
like a banty rooster through the
high school locker room, hardballed
biceps, humongous cock abob. Jesus,
he had a handsome face, black hair
Brillianteened.

Yesterday I heard Donald Lee
was dead. And I thought, Thank God
I'll never have to go to class reunion
and see Donald Lee Smith toothless,
or with dentures, bald as an egg.
In my mind he'll strut, strut, strut.

How I Missed Seeing Judy Garland

When I was a young teenager
one of my idols was Judy Garland.
(She still is.) I had the 78s.

One day I read in the *Philadelphia
Inquirer* that she was appearing
at The Palace Theatre in New York.

I saved my allowances and sent
my Aunt Elinor in Manhattan
a twenty-five dollar mail order.

"Get me the Saturday matinee ticket,"
I wrote. Then I bought a bus ticket.
On the Greyhound my head was full

of *Sewanee, You Made Me Love You*,
and especially *Over the Rainbow*,
with its happy little bluebirds.

When I got to New York,
my aunt said proudly, "Oh,
that's only a one-woman show

on a bare stage. I bought you
a ticket for a real Broadway
musical—choruses! Scenery!"

It was something called
Texas 'Lil Darling with
someone named Kenny Delmar.

I hated every minute of it.
Years later, when Garland died,
I went up to Frank Campbell's

Funeral Parlor for the viewing.
But the line went on for blocks.
That's how I missed seeing Judy Garland again.

The Four Seasons
Il cimento dell'armonia e dell'invenzione.
—Antonio Vivaldi

I.

Spring tumbles down
like circus clowns
from a trick automobile.
Red, yellow, blue blurs
spill over the ground.
The air fills with zany
beauty. No Barnum and Bailey
more spectacular, spring
juggles, rides a dapple
bareback beneath a tent
of blue, walks a silver
high wire without any net,
waves, teeters, trips,
then plunges through
the summer air straight
toward a hard cool fall.

II.

Slow as the rhetoric of Warren G. Harding,
summer staggers to its knees, stunned
as a poleaxed steer at slaughter.
Beside the highway, vegetable stands groan,
sweet corn, peaches lolling like Rubens' nudes,
tomatoes red as Red Cross plasma.
In the fields, scarecrows are empty-headed
uncles. Ponds shadow green as Canada
geese fly by. Sand congregates in swimsuit crotches.
Day lilies trumpet the garden's four corners,
black-eyed Susans meet the day's eye,
loosestrife floods the marshes with fire.

Chipmunks assume the shape of pears,
snakes snooze and dream of shrews,
robins bob for worms like apples in a barrel.
Air conditioners wheeze, captive dolphins;
dust-pussies lie under country beds.
Crickets, domesticated Vivaldis.
Night drops, a lady's chemise, not too clean.
Insects, both sexes, dive-bomb the porch light.
The planet, like love, slowly turns to ice.

III.

November fifteenth, and still no fall
of leaves. They cling tenaciously
to every branch and stem. Weeks ago
they turned color, now turncoat
and will not let go. Even last night's
Sturm und Drang left them unperturbed.
In the country the bushel baskets
are impatient, awaiting their legacies,
their windfalls. Wheelbarrows stand
unmoving. Each suburban garage and cellar
house rakes and yard brooms, which lean
upon one another like mourning next of kin.
Gutters at rooflines are amazed:
Each autumn they strangle on leaves—
yet last night's rain set them singing
clear and high, a castrati choir.
All the baseballs boys lost last summer
long to be blanketed down for winter.
Will the leaves never fall?
Will this be the fall that failed?

IV.

Shadows, thin, blue, razor sharp.
Shadows, cutting crust, mummy mush.
Silence lies like a white sheet
over the dead, the earth a rigid cadaver.
The sun, a withered yellow apple,
shines but does not warm the glazed land.
The muteness of the universe,
a gash in the head of a bass drum.
Cold laps and licks bare bone,
enters, like an unwelcome guest,
into cracks and crevices vainly stuffed
with oily rags, wadded newspapers.
Until a storm of snowbirds
whirl and screech above frozen forests,
freezing beaks seeking sustenance,
as if heralding the almost-ready rise
of spring. All nature stands poised—
a young woman before her drawn bath—
tiptoes on the edge of warmth,
the gay splashing of this our life.